**INTRODUCING
ISSUES WITH
OPPOSING
VIEWPOINTS®**

Sports and Athletes

Noël Merino, *Book Editor*

GREENHAVEN PRESS
A part of Gale, Cengage Learning

GALE
CENGAGE Learning™

Detroit • New York • San Francisco • New Haven, Conn • Waterville, Maine • London

Christine Nasso, *Publisher*
Elizabeth Des Chenes, *Managing Editor*

LIBRARY OF CONGRESS CATALOGING-IN-PUBLICATION DATA

Sports and athletes / Noël Merino, book editor.
    p. cm. -- (Introducing issues with opposing viewpoints)
  Includes bibliographical references and index.
  ISBN 978-0-7377-4942-7 (hardcover)
  1. Sports. 2. Athletes. I. Merino, Noël.
  GV565.S66 2010
  796--dc22

                                                          2010004956

Printed in the United States of America
1 2 3 4 5 6 7 14 13 12 11 10

Contents

Chapter 3: Should College Sports Be Reformed?

Foreword

Indulging in a wide spectrum of ideas, beliefs, and perspectives is a critical cornerstone of democracy. After all, it is often debates over differences of opinion, such as whether to legalize abortion, how to treat prisoners, or when to enact the death penalty, that shape our society and drive it forward. Such diversity of thought is frequently regarded as the hallmark of a healthy and civilized culture. As the Reverend Clifford Schutjer of the First Congregational Church in Mansfield, Ohio, declared in a 2001 sermon, "Surrounding oneself with only like-minded people, restricting what we listen to or read only to what we find agreeable is irresponsible. Refusing to entertain doubts once we make up our minds is a subtle but deadly form of arrogance." With this advice in mind, Introducing Issues with Opposing Viewpoints books aim to open readers' minds to the critically divergent views that comprise our world's most important debates.

Introducing Issues with Opposing Viewpoints simplifies for students the enormous and often overwhelming mass of material now available via print and electronic media. Collected in every volume is an array of opinions that captures the essence of a particular controversy or topic. Introducing Issues with Opposing Viewpoints books embody the spirit of nineteenth-century journalist Charles A. Dana's axiom: "Fight for your opinions, but do not believe that they contain the whole truth, or the only truth." Absorbing such contrasting opinions teaches students to analyze the strength of an argument and compare it to its opposition. From this process readers can inform and strengthen their own opinions, or be exposed to new information that will change their minds. Introducing Issues with Opposing Viewpoints is a mosaic of different voices. The authors are statesmen, pundits, academics, journalists, corporations, and ordinary people who have felt compelled to share their experiences and ideas in a public forum. Their words have been collected from newspapers, journals, books, speeches, interviews, and the Internet, the fastest growing body of opinionated material in the world.

Introducing Issues with Opposing Viewpoints shares many of the well-known features of its critically acclaimed parent series, Opposing Viewpoints. The articles are presented in a pro/con format, allowing readers to absorb divergent perspectives side by side. Active reading questions preface each viewpoint, requiring the student to approach the material thoughtfully and carefully. Useful charts, graphs, and cartoons supplement each article. A thorough introduction provides readers with crucial background on an issue. An annotated bibliography points the reader toward articles, books, and Web sites that contain additional information on the topic. An appendix of organizations to contact contains a wide variety of charities, nonprofit organizations, political groups, and private enterprises that each hold a position on the issue at hand. Finally, a comprehensive index allows readers to locate content quickly and efficiently.

Introducing Issues with Opposing Viewpoints is also significantly different from Opposing Viewpoints. As the series title implies, its presentation will help introduce students to the concept of opposing viewpoints, and learn to use this material to aid in critical writing and debate. The series' four-color, accessible format makes the books attractive and inviting to readers of all levels. In addition, each viewpoint has been carefully edited to maximize a reader's understanding of the content. Short but thorough viewpoints capture the essence of an argument. A substantial, thought-provoking essay question placed at the end of each viewpoint asks the student to further investigate the issues raised in the viewpoint, compare and contrast two authors' arguments, or consider how one might go about forming an opinion on the topic at hand. Each viewpoint contains sidebars that include at-a-glance information and handy statistics. A Facts About section located in the back of the book further supplies students with relevant facts and figures.

Following in the tradition of the Opposing Viewpoints series, Greenhaven Press continues to provide readers with invaluable exposure to the controversial issues that shape our world. As John Stuart Mill once wrote: "The only way in which a human being can make some approach to knowing the whole of a subject is by hearing what can be said about it by persons of every variety of opinion and studying all modes in which it can be looked at by every character of mind. No wise man ever acquired his wisdom in any mode but this." It is to this principle that Introducing Issues with Opposing Viewpoints books are dedicated.

Introduction

Sports are extremely popular in the United States. According to a 2009 Gallup poll, 56 percent of U.S. adults describe themselves as sports fans.[1] And according to the National Federation of State High School Associations, 55 percent of high school students participate in high school sports.[2] The Bureau of Labor Statistics of the U.S. Department of Labor reported in its 2008 American Time Use Survey that 18 percent of adults spend between one and two hours a day participating in sports, exercise, and recreation.[3] According to the Nielsen Company, 2009 was a record-breaking year for U.S. sports television: the most-viewed Super Bowl game in history, the most-viewed Stanley Cup game in seven years, and the most-viewed World Series in five years. Given this popularity of sports in mainstream culture, it is no wonder that athletes are often revered.

This admiration and elevation of athletes, however, can have a dark side, as athletes are often not held responsible for their actions in the same way others are. The 2000–2001 University of Washington football team, winner of the Rose Bowl in 2001, had several examples of athletes who may have engaged in criminal behavior that was overlooked because of their performance on the athletic field for a winning team. The issue of college athletes appearing to be treated as above the law and, perhaps as such, engaging in an unusual amount of criminal activity, is a problem that is not limited to the University of Washington, but the amount of controversy created during the 2000–2001 season was remarkable.

During the summer of 2000, Jerramy Stevens was heading into his junior year as a tight end for the University of Washington Huskies and considered one of their best players, likely to be a top National Football League (NFL) draft pick. In July 2000 Stevens was arrested on suspicion of drugging a nineteen-year-old freshman at a fraternity party and raping her in an alley. In October prosecutors decided not to charge Stevens in that case, saying a four-month investigation had failed to produce sufficient evidence to support the allegation: Although DNA evidence existed, Stevens claims to have engaged in consensual sex whereas the freshman alleged that she was drugged and raped. Detective Maryann Parker believes that Stevens should have been charged with the rape, stating, "I think we just felt, in our unit and in the Police Department as a whole, that this case was handled differently. And we felt it was because he was a University of Washington football star."[4] Stevens has maintained his innocence regarding the rape, though he has had several other run-ins with the law since—mainly involving drinking and driving. In 2003 the freshman woman who accused him of rape filed a civil lawsuit against Stevens, the University of Washington, and the Sigma Chi fraternity, where she believed she had been slipped a date-rape drug. Stevens and the fraternity settled with the woman. Stevens currently is tight end for the NFL team Tampa Bay Buccaneers.

Jeremiah Pharms was a star linebacker for the University of Washington Huskies, helping the Huskies win the Rose Bowl during his final year. Pharms was drafted by the NFL team Cleveland Browns in the spring of 2001, but before signing his contract he was arrested and charged for a crime committed nearly fourteen months prior. In March 2000 a marijuana dealer had been robbed, beaten, and shot. Eyewitness and physical evidence linked Pharms to the crime, but police failed to charge Pharms until after the 2000–2001 season. In the end, Pharms was only charged with robbery and sentenced to three years and five months. The judge in the case remarked, "It's difficult to imagine a more serious robbery without it becoming an attempted-murder conviction."[5] Since his release in 2004, he has been charged with two felonies.

Curtis Williams played football for the University of Washington from 1996 to 2000. Although Williams was arrested for assaulting his wife several times throughout those years, he kept his scholarship and only lost playtime during one year when a jail sentence made it impossible for him to stay in classes. Williams was paralyzed during a football game in October 2000 and died in 2002. Throughout the media coverage of his football career and beyond, his criminal history of assault was rarely ever mentioned or discussed.

One concern about the popularity of sport in American culture is that athletes may sometimes be treated as above the law. This is one of the many concerns about the place of sport in society and the place of athletes. Among the many debated concerns, the issues of whether sports and athletes have a positive impact on society, whether the use of performance-enhancing drugs by athletes is a problem, and whether college sports should be reformed are explored in *Introducing Issues with Opposing Viewpoints: Sports and Athletes.*

Notes

1. Gallup poll, August 6–9, 2009. www.gallup.com/poll/4735/Sports .aspx#1.
2. National Federation of State High School Associations, "High School Sports Participation Increases for 20th Consecutive Year," September 15, 2009. www.nfhs.org/content.aspx?id=3505.
3. Bureau of Labor Statistics, "Table 2: Time Spent in Primary Activities," June 24, 2009. www.bls.gov/news.release/atus.t02.htm.
4. Quoted in Ken Armstrong and Nick Perry, "Victory and Ruins: Chapter 1," *Seattle Times*, January 27, 2008. http://seattletimes.nw source.com/html/victoryandruins.
5. Quoted in Armstrong and Perry, "Victory and Ruins: Chapter 2."

Chapter 1

Do Sports and Athletes Have a Positive Impact on Society?

The spectacle, excitement, and rivalry of modern sporting events have made them a popular pastime for most people.

Viewpoint

1

Sports Are a Civilized Way to Express Rivalry

Windsor Mann

"Domestic obsession with team sports is a positive sign; it suggests that war-torn rivals have found a safe venue in which to settle the score."

In the following viewpoint Windsor Mann argues that sports are a healthy way to channel tribal aggression. By identifying with a team and the other fans of that team, rivalry is expressed toward other teams but without any of the costs of the kind of real rivalry found in war. Mann claims that widespread athletics in a country indicates that the country has moved from the dangerous rivalry of war to the civilized rivalry of sports. Mann is a writer who frequently contributes to the *American Spectator* and the *Washington Times*.

Windsor Mann, "Playing (War) Games," *National Review Online*, February 7, 2006. Copyright © 2006 by National Review, Inc., 215 Lexington Avenue, New York, NY 10016. Reproduced by permission.

AS YOU READ, CONSIDER THE FOLLOWING QUESTIONS:

1. According to the author, people become sports fans in order to do what?
2. Mann claims that although athletic competition itself may not end hostilities within a country, it may indicate what?
3. The author suggests that football became popular as a substitute for what?

A fter watching Super Bowl XL on Sunday night [February 5, 2006], I got to thinking. Since my team, the Indianapolis Colts, did not qualify for the game, I was able to think rationally, even sociologically and philosophically, about what it all meant—football, that is.

The Athletic Clan

Looking at both sides' fans, I couldn't help but notice that there really wasn't much to notice. Both sides look the same, speak the same language, and lead similar lives. Like any NFL [National Football League] fans, they just happen to root for different colors and mascots. In the grand scheme of things, nothing separates [Pittsburgh] Steelers fans from [Seattle] Seahawks fans other than a couple of time zones. Which raises the question: Why do they pull for different teams? How can people so similar have conflicting loyalties? More generally, why are there even fans to begin with?

As strange as this may sound, people become fans in order to become part of a tribe—each with its own customs, chants, costumes, and idiosyncrasies. America, like Iraq today or Scotland centuries ago, is still a tribal society, but a highly sophisticated one. Sectarian conflict still exists, but it is artificial and superficial and, thankfully, governed by officials. We no longer fight with weapons; now we fight with footballs. Instead of fighting to the death, we play until sudden death. Unlike our brethren in the Middle East, Americans have learned how to channel their tribal aggression. That channel is ESPN.

The beauty of team sports is that they allow us, as fans, to identify with a large group of people—mostly strangers—who partake in a common heritage, cheering on players we will never meet. In this way, being a fan is no different than being a tribesman. Singing the fight songs, donning the colors, and investing one's time, money and emotion in a team's success—these are the ways of the athletic clan.

Sports and Conflict

Yet, what works inside a country doesn't necessarily work between countries. The Olympics haven't yet proved to be a cure for war. Recreational softball won't keep Kim Jong Il [leader of North Korea] from playing nuclear hardball, just as field hockey isn't going to cajole Hamas [Palestinian Islamic movement] into coexistence with Israel (evidently suicide bombers don't like the idea of short-skirted girls who speak softly and carry big sticks).

Believing that a sports league is the answer to global conflict is about the same as believing the

League of Nations [a precurser to the United Nations] is. Similarly, sports cannot end sectarian conflict in Iraq any more than the United

Sports allow fans to identify with large groups of people in a common interest that allows them to become part of a "tribe."

Nations could prevent America from invading it. [UN secretary general] Kofi Annan cannot referee the world into peace.

Nevertheless, while athletic competition itself may not be a remedy for ending hostilities, sometimes it indicates that hostilities may already be ebbing.

When the teams represent significant blocs of society, sports can serve as a medium for enmity between rival factions within a country. More often than not, domestic obsession with team sports is a positive sign; it suggests that war-torn rivals have found a safe venue in which to settle the score.

A Sign of Civilization

It is worth noting that American football became popular in the late 19th century—after a war that had divided the nation against itself and pitted brother against brother. Writer Jim Weeks suggests that in those volatile postwar years, football emerged as a substitute for war. "In an era concerned with reviving the Civil War virtues of self-sacrifice, courage, discipline, teamwork and public spirit, football appeared to be the panacea."

That the teams in the NFL and NCAA [National Collegiate Athletic Association] represent major cities or states shows how civilized and harmonious American society has become. Better for Carolina and New York to face off on the gridiron than in civil war.

> **FAST FACT**
>
> According to Nielsen Media Research, the Super Bowl was the most-watched TV broadcast of the year each year from 2000 to 2009, garnering almost 100 million viewers for Super Bowl XLIII in 2009.

The same fighting spirit that pervaded America in 1861 persists to this day in stadiums across the country. Thanks to football, secession is no longer necessary, but a Lombardi trophy [given to the winning team of the Super Bowl] is.

Even when we pretend that a game is a life-and-death matter, we suffer none of the costs of war. We get the excitement but none of the pain—at least not the sort that Shiites and Sunnis are now experiencing.

Average Percent of Americans Identifying as Sports Fans, 1993–2006

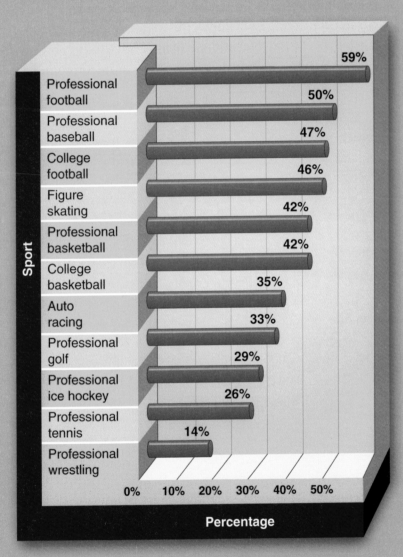

Taken from: Jeffrey M. Jones, "Nearly Half of Americas Are Baseball Fans," Gallup, April 4, 2006.

In the end, it doesn't matter whether Iraq's major factions ever find reconciliation. What matters is how they express their animosity.

[English novelist and journalist] George Orwell once described sport as "war minus the shooting," which, if true, would be a welcome improvement in Iraq and elsewhere.

We will know Iraq has reached maturity as a civil society when the main topic of conversation among Sunnis, Kurds and Shiites is who among them is winning—not in the parliamentary elections, not on the battlefield, but on the athletic field. The turning point will come when they put down their shotguns and go into shotgun formation.

> ## EVALUATING THE AUTHORS' ARGUMENTS:
>
> In this viewpoint Mann argues that obsession with team sports is a positive sign. In what way does Zimmerman, the author of the next viewpoint, disagree with this view?

The Place of Sports in American Culture Is Too Extreme

Jonathan Zimmerman

"Americans are addicted to competitive sports in ways that are profoundly unhealthy to our schools, our bodies, and ourselves."

In the following viewpoint Jonathan Zimmerman argues that America has a harmful addiction to sports. He contends that an obsession with sports has caused schools to make poor decisions about school schedules and school employee salaries. He also argues that sports are dangerous to youth by promoting drug use and unreported injuries. Although Zimmerman concedes that sports can have a positive place in culture, he concludes that their current place in American culture is one of dangerous excess. Zimmerman is professor of education and history and director of the History of Education Program in the Steinhardt School of Culture, Education, and Human Development at New York University.

1. According to the author, U.S. high schools start the day at 7:30 AM for what reason?
2. The average weight of American Olympic gymnasts has decreased by how many pounds between 1976 and 1992, according to Zimmerman?
3. The author contends that anonymous player questionnaires show that the percentage of football players who have suffered concussions is what?

L ast week [November 2007], when a federal grand jury indicted baseball star Barry Bonds for perjury, it confirmed an ugly truth: America's got a big drug problem.

America's Addiction

I'm not talking about steroids, Mr. Bonds' alleged performance-enhancer of choice. Instead, I'm talking about athletics themselves. Americans are addicted to competitive sports in ways that are profoundly unhealthy to our schools, our bodies, and ourselves. And until we confront that problem, head-on, steroids will continue to plague us.

Consider this simple fact: Although every shred of evidence shows that adolescents do not learn well before 9 A.M., US high schools start the day at around 7:30 A.M. Why? To make room for afternoon sports practice, of course. And consider that the time allotted to athletic practice—often two or three hours—is much longer than any academic class period.

Most high schools allot between two-thirds and three-quarters of their extracurricular budgets to sports. In his bestselling book, *Friday Night Lights*, since adapted into a movie and television series, H.G. Bissinger reported that a Texas high school spent more on football game film than it did on teaching materials for the English department. The team's coach earned 50 percent more than a regular classroom teacher with 20 years experience.

In the great college-admissions sweepstakes, recruited high school athletes get twice the advantage that racial minorities receive. But while many Americans squeal about affirmative action for blacks or

Hispanics, nobody blinks an eye at special passes for the quarterback or power forward.

Ah, you might say, but these athletes are overwhelmingly minorities themselves. False. As every single study has shown, the vast majority of recruited athletes are white teens from well-to-do families. And these families use their privilege to buy services—coaches, trainers, and summer camps—to ensure that they get a leg up. So much for the level playing field.

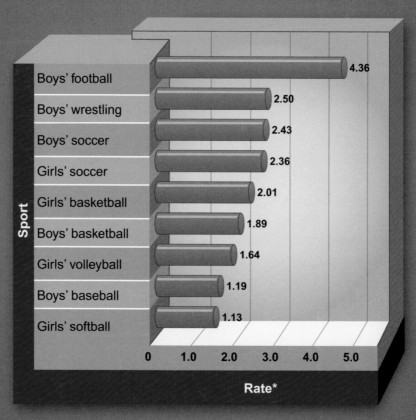

Sports-Specific Injury Rates in United States High School Sports

Sport	Rate*
Boys' football	4.36
Boys' wrestling	2.50
Boys' soccer	2.43
Girls' soccer	2.36
Girls' basketball	2.01
Boys' basketball	1.89
Girls' volleyball	1.64
Boys' baseball	1.19
Girls' softball	1.13

*Per 1,000 athlete exposures (i.e. practices or competitions).

Taken from: Centers for Disease Control and Prevention, "Sports-Related Injuries Among High School Athletes—United States, 2005–06 School Year," Mortality and Morbidity Weekly Review, vol. 55, 2006, p. 1038.

Young gymnasts are increasingly plagued by eating disorders. The average weight of a female gymnast has decreased from 106 pounds in 1976 to 83 pounds in 1992.

The Dangers of Sports

But sports help our kids stay fit and healthy, right? Sure. But competitive athletics can harm young bodies, too. Think of girls' gymnastics, which has witnessed a spate of eating disorders. In 1976, America's Olympic gymnasts averaged 106 pounds each; by 1992, their average weight was down to 83 pounds. And if you think that's all because of healthy dieting, well, I've got an amphetamine pill to sell you.

The most dangerous sport is football, of course. During the past decade, at least 50 high school or junior-high-school players have been killed or have sustained serious head injuries on the field. Some of these deaths could have been prevented if we took the risk more seriously.

But we don't. Although athletic trainers report that 5 percent of high school football players have a concussion each season, anonymous player questionnaires bring the number up to 15 percent. And when the word "concussion" is omitted and a list of symptoms is provided instead, nearly half of all players report that they have sustained a concussion.

So why don't they tell their coaches? We all know the answer: They want to play. And they want to win.

That's the same reason they take

steroids, even in the face of drug tests. A new two-year study of 11 Oregon high schools—based, again, on questionnaires of the players—showed that random drug testing did nothing to deter steroid use.

And yet we continue to ratchet up the drug tests, instead of ratcheting down our addiction to sports. The governor of Texas, Rick Perry (R), recently signed a bill allowing the testing of all high school athletes, setting aside $3 million per year for the tests. But every single dollar will go to waste as long as we teach our kids that we value athletics —and victory—above everything else.

A Harm of Excess

Full disclosure: I play sports. I watch sports. I *love* sports. Like most things, however, sports are harmful in excess. And that's exactly the case at every level of athletics in America.

A century ago, all high school athletics were organized and managed by the students themselves. Then the adults took over. Schools hired coaches, provided uniforms, built new gymnasiums, and so on. And they made the athletes—especially the boys—into the unofficial kings of the institution.

That brings us back to Barry Bonds, the nation's flawed home run champion. It's easy to condemn him for possibly cheating his way into the record books. But part of that condemnation ought to be directed at ourselves, too, because many of us would have done the same thing—if we knew we could get away with it. When the whole culture tells you that sports rule, nobody will follow the rules around sports.

> **EVALUATING THE AUTHORS' ARGUMENTS:**
>
> In this viewpoint Zimmerman claims that the American obsession with sports is harmful. How might Mann, author of the previous viewpoint, respond to Zimmerman's allegation?

Youth Sports Have Numerous Benefits

Brooke de Lench

"The goal should be full inclusion: Nobody gets cut from the team."

In the following viewpoint Brooke de Lench argues that greater inclusion of young people in organized after-school sports would have a variety of positive benefits. She argues that a necessary part of pursuing such a goal would be to adopt a policy of inclusion of all students who want to play sports in middle school and high school. De Lench argues that greater participation in sports would have numerous benefits for young people, including greater fitness, better academic performance, and a sense of belonging. De Lench is the author of *Home Team Advantage: The Critical Role of Mothers in Youth Sports* and editor in chief of Moms Team.com, an online publication for mothers parenting children active in youth sports.

AS YOU READ, CONSIDER THE FOLLOWING QUESTIONS:
  1. The current public high school model of sports was adopted approximately how many years ago, according to the author?
  2. According to de Lench, what fraction of teens is now overweight?
  3. The author proposes that under a new system of full inclusion, which athletes would practice and which athletes would suit up for games?

O
ne of the most important things that government could do to reduce drug use, fight the obesity epidemic and deal with a host of other youth problems is quite simple: Include more kids in organized after-school sports.

Sports for All

But to do that, we must first make some major changes in interscholastic sports programs in the nation's public middle and high schools. The goal should be full inclusion: Nobody gets cut from the team.

The current public high school model—one first-year team, one varsity, maybe one sub-varsity—might have made sense when it was adopted some 80 years ago. Back then, in many schools the number of roster spots on a team was roughly equal to the number who wanted to play. But it makes no sense today, when the number of those who want to continue playing sports in middle school and high school far exceeds the finite number of spots available.

The Benefits of Full Inclusion

According to a Gallup Youth Study in February [2006], one in five teens is now overweight, and only one in five teens say they participate in sports or recreation five to six days a week.

Obviously, young people who are cut from sports teams aren't likely to exercise as frequently as they would if they were playing sports; they're much more likely to spend their afternoons watching television, becoming obese and perhaps getting into trouble.

Another recent study found a positive association between a teenager playing interscholastic sports and the number of his or her friends who are academically oriented. The study also found that participation in interscholastic sports "significantly increased social ties between students and parents, students and the school, parents and the school, and parents and parents" and brought about "a reduction in illicit drug and alcohol use."

It's especially important for teenagers to know that they belong, that they fit in. Cutting teenagers from sports teams tells them that they don't fit in. It's the wrong message to send during adolescence.

As the most prominent of all high school extracurricular activities, athletics continues to confer on its participants the highest levels of status and prestige in our teenage culture. The feeling among athletes that they are special tends to lead to disharmony in schools, to the creation of cliques and to reinforcement of the jock culture. It undermines the feelings of community, full inclusion and cooperative learning that schools work so hard to instill.

Adopting a policy of full inclusion would be especially beneficial for teenage boys, for whom sports provide an outlet for aggression and a means of connecting socially with other boys.

In the United States one in five teens is overweight, and only one in five participates in sports or recreational exercise five to six days a week.

Ten Most Popular Sports Programs, by Participants

Boys

Sport	Number of Participants
1. Football – 11 player	1,112,303
2. Track and Field – Outdoor	558,007
3. Basketball	545,145
4. Baseball	473,184
5. Soccer	383,824
6. Wrestling	267,378
7. Cross Country	231,452
8. Tennis	157,165
9. Golf	157,062
10. Swimming and Diving	130,182

Girls

Sport	Number of Participants
1. Track and Field – Outdoor	457,732
2. Basketball	444,809
3. Volleyball	404,243
4. Softball – Fast Pitch	368,921
5. Soccer	344,534
6. Cross Country	198,199
7. Tennis	177,593
8. Swimming and Diving	158,878
9. Competitive Spirit Squads	117,793
10. Golf	69,223

Taken from: National Federation of State High School Associations, "2008–09 Athletics Participation Summary," 2009. www.nfhs.org.

Adding Teams to Meet Demand

Under a system of full inclusion, teams would be added as necessary to meet the demand, even if it meant fielding, say, two or three junior varsity basketball teams. Every athlete would practice, but only those with good academic standing, good attendance records and no disciplinary problems would suit up for games. To ensure that schools would field the most competitive teams, the most skilled players would still get the bulk of the playing time at the varsity level. But no one would be cut.

The extra teams could be at least partially funded through additional user fees, with money raised by booster clubs, by donations from local businesses and by the parents of the athletes themselves, some of whom could be recruited as volunteer coaches.

Not only would full inclusion for school sports help our kids, it would eliminate one of the principal reasons for parental misbehavior in youth sports. Given the intense competition for limited roster spots on high school teams, no wonder so many parents are led by our winner-take-all society to act in inappropriate ways—to become violent when they see their child's chances at winning one of the coveted spots threatened by a coach who decides to sit him or her on the bench.

It makes no sense from a public health standpoint to continue a policy that contributes to an overall decline in physical fitness among adolescents and young adults and does nothing to combat drug use by keeping teens busy in after-school programs such as sports.

EVALUATING THE AUTHORS' ARGUMENTS:

In this viewpoint de Lench argues that all students in middle school and high school who want to play sports should get to play. What concerns would McIntosh, author of the next viewpoint, have about de Lench's proposal?

Viewpoint

4

Youth Sports Can Be Harmful

Tara McIntosh

"The number one reason kids drop out of sports is because they're no longer fun."

In the following viewpoint Tara McIntosh argues that children are specializing in sports much too early. McIntosh contends that one danger with this kind of approach to sports is that sports are less fun to play, causing young people to quit. A more concrete danger, she claims, is that intense training at a young age puts children at risk for serious injuries. She concludes by encouraging parents to keep sports fun for their children and support a variety of different athletic pursuits. McIntosh writes a monthly column for *The Tri-City News*, a newspaper in British Columbia, Canada.

"Too serious too soon." That's what one coach said when I asked him: "Why do you think 70% of kids drop out of sports by the time they're 13?"

"They're being developed in sports too young," he said, "so they'll burn out. And this one-sport-only-all-year-long nonsense is a guarantee they'll get bored and suffer some serious overuse injuries, too."

The Trend Toward Specialization

Coach has a point. And according to *Sports Illustrated*, the number one reason kids drop out of sports is because they're no longer fun.

The problem? A small group of probably well-meaning parents or coaches who insist on time-consuming, physically draining development teams for kids who are too young.

About 12 years ago, a generation of parents experienced an athletic epiphany that would define how the next generation of children would be raised. It was the international introduction of Tiger Woods and those now famous "flashback" TV clips of a two-year-old Tiger playing golf on the Michael Douglas show [The Mike Douglas Show]. Unquestionably, this image would cook the recipe for success into the minds of every helicopter parent alive: Start them young, specialize in one sport and hover at every tryout, game and tournament.

> **FAST FACT**
>
> According to the American Orthopaedic Society for Sports Medicine, American children suffer an estimated 2 million sports-related injuries each year, resulting in 500,000 doctor visits and 30,000 hospitalizations.

The payoff? A smiling you on the sidelines, your kid's face on a cereal box, mortgage paid or, at the very least, a sports scholarship.

The Dangers of Early Specialization

The reality? Intense practice schedules that rarely leave 12-year-olds enough time to get their homework done, a 20% increase in serious overuse injuries in kids under 15 (such as damaged growth plates and ACLs [anterior cruciate ligaments]) and a generation of "trophy kids" who'd like their parents to stop acting like a bunch of agents.

In his book, *Until It Hurts: America's Obsession with Youth Sports and How It Harms Our Kids*, author Mark Hyman blames adults and their sometimes self-serving interference in youth sports for many kids quitting. He also interviews countless professionals who agree that early specialization in a sport wreaks havoc on a young athlete's body.

Dr. Jane T. Servi, a sports medicine specialist, said children need "a rotation and variety of sports to develop their whole bodies and avoid the overuse of any one muscle."

It should be noted that Brazilian soccer legend Pelé started playing soccer at 11 and started on a development team at 15.

And in a *National Post* interview, The Great One, [Canadian professional ice hockey player] Wayne Gretzky, said, "The worst thing to happen to the game of hockey has been year-round hockey. Athletes can only learn by mixing up games they play when they're young . . . I could hardly wait to get my lacrosse stick out."

The Requirement for Fun

Unfortunately, with North America's newly adopted Eastern Bloc approach to building young athletes (which includes zero resting time in between a change of sports), kids don't always get this opportunity. Ironically, many children who were trained exactly the same way decades earlier escaped to North America for a little fun and freedom.

So what do we do, parents? Don't buy into it. Because while the majority of coaches and parents are rounded regarding youth sports, you'll always have your type A's [personality type] who push kids before they're developmentally ready and that's when they burn out and hurt themselves.

And, yes, while I know times have changed, children's requirement for fun never will.

Critics say children are participating in rigorous athletic training that puts them at risk for serious injuries.

Someone once said that children between the ages of 12 and 17 can age a parent 20 years. I'm thinking 13-year-olds who keep playing soccer—and lacrosse and baseball and whatever else they like—instead of hanging out in convenience store parking lots could slow that process.

EVALUATING THE AUTHORS' ARGUMENTS:

In this viewpoint McIntosh claims that children should pursue a variety of sports without intense training. Could both McIntosh and de Lench, author of the previous viewpoint, agree on this point? Why or why not?

Athletes Should Be Considered Role Models

Daniel B. Wood

"Children also choose their role models apart from their parents' suggestions."

Daniel B. Wood discusses the reactions of different young people to the news of Tiger Woods's affairs and provides some advice on how parents can help their children deal with the failure of a role model to provide a good example to follow. Though Woods has not claimed to be a role model, parents and children around the world have made him one. The author cites a number of authorities who offer suggestions about how to use such role-model failures as opportunities to teach children valuable lessons about life and to find out how the children are handling the news about the role model.

Daniel B. Wood is a staff writer for *The Christian Science Monitor*.

Daniel B. Wood, "Kids React to Tiger Woods Apology. How Can Parents Talk About It?" *The Christian Science Monitor*, February 19, 2010. Copyright © 2010 *The Christian Science Monitor*. All Rights Reserved. Reproduced by permission.

AS YOU READ, CONSIDER THE FOLLOWING QUESTIONS:

1. Who is Jim Fannin and how does he suggest that parents approach the problem of failure of a role model, according to the author?
2. Who are Esther Latique and Dr. Joni Fraser and what message do they want children to hear when a role model fails, according to the viewpoint?
3. Who is Carleton Kendrick, and what advice does he have for parents when dealing with bad behavior by a role model, as mentioned by the author?

"I'm pretty bummed about it," says Terry, tapping in a three-foot putt. "Here was a guy sitting on top of the world because of the control he demonstrated on the golf course. Why couldn't that control cross over into his personal life? It makes him suspect to me."

"It doesn't bother me at all," says Sammy. "What a guy does outside his sphere of excellence is just not important to me. He can still be my hero and someone I want to be like."

The comments frame two sides of a debate that has erupted with Woods's 1,511-word apology Friday, read before a small gathering of friends and colleagues, but carried live across the globe.

He said, "I knew my actions were wrong, but I convinced myself that normal rules didn't apply. I never thought about who I was hurting; instead, I thought only about myself."

The world's most highly paid sports star is also the role model for millions of youths around the world, a topic that is now bubbling to the surface after months of Woods's silence about his infidelities.

No matter what your personal opinion of his extramarital behavior—or the way he has handled it publicly—the episode is the perfect "teachable moment," say a host of sociologists, relationship experts, and sports psychologists.

"Role models don't have to be perfect," says Jim Fannin, a 35-year author, educator, and platform speaker who has coached several Olympic gold medalists and PGA golfers, among others.

"I really believe that he is still capable of passing on lessons to kids. Being a champion is about getting up one more time from defeat and moving on with focus. That is what he is doing."

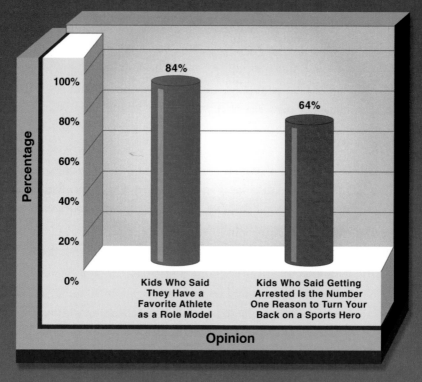

Kids on Athletes as Role Models

Percentage

100%
80%
60%
40%
20%
0%

84%

64%

Kids Who Said
They Have a
Favorite Athlete
as a Role Model

Kids Who Said Getting
Arrested Is the Number
One Reason to Turn Your
Back on a Sports Hero

Opinion

Taken from: Ron Berler, "Fallen Heroes: Bad Behavior by Some of Your Favorite Sports Stars Made Us Wonder If You Still Trust Athletes to Be Role Models. Here's What You Told Us," *Sports Illustrated for Kids*, vol. 17, no. 5, May 1, 2005, p.48.

The past decade has seen a blurring of the line between fame and excellence, Mr. Fannin says. "Kids looking up to superstars today see more about the trappings of success than the essence of it," Fannin says. "They see guys pictured as drinking Gatorade and wearing Nike shoes and then think, 'When I get to be great, that's what it will be like.' This shows there is obviously more to being a champion than that. This is the lesson to be learned here."

Authors and relationship consultants Esther Latique and Dr. Joni Fraser say the Woods episode has exposed children to a very dangerous message—that the rules that apply to everyone don't apply to our heroes. "It's even harder when we have to explain behaviors that we don't condone and don't want them to emulate," they say.

That's why they feel it is good that Woods stated, "I ran straight through the boundaries that married people should live by. I thought I could get away with whatever I wanted to. . . . I don't get to play by different rules."

Parents should go on the offensive, says Susan Bartell, author of the new book series, "Top 50 Questions Kids Ask."

She suggests asking open-ended questions like, "What did you hear?" or "What do you think about it?" which can reveal how much the child really understands and how the child is feeling emotionally. Also, making it a conversation rather than a lecture is a more effective way to communicate.

"Helping your child understand the distinction between poor choices and bad people is also key," she says. "And once you've helped your child make sense of these adult issues, it's important to explain to your kids that their actions don't make them any less of an athlete and they can still appreciate what they did in the sport. Using this incident as a teachable moment will lead children to a better understanding of what's acceptable and what's not. The more parents speak to their kids about these hot-button topics, the more likely they are to have effective communication with them."

Fannin, who has played golf with Woods several times, has studied Buddhism, and knows the Thai culture, says Woods's biggest hurdle will be overcoming family shame.

"I watched his mother during his apology, and she was sitting with crossed arms, showing her disgust," he says. "They hugged, but she was still ashamed . . . and when you shame a family in Thailand, it's a very big deal, indeed."

Many felt that Woods was sincere and went very far in his apology. Others felt he was too scripted and did not go far enough.

Family therapist Carleton Kendrick says the biggest shock has come because of the differences between Woods's carefully crafted persona and his real self.

"Woods has never, to my knowledge, publicly stated that he is [or] should be a role model for children 'the world over.' His PR and marketing team have carefully orchestrated an 'All-American,' family man, public persona for him designed to appeal to both men and women, families, children and parents," says Mr. Kendrick.

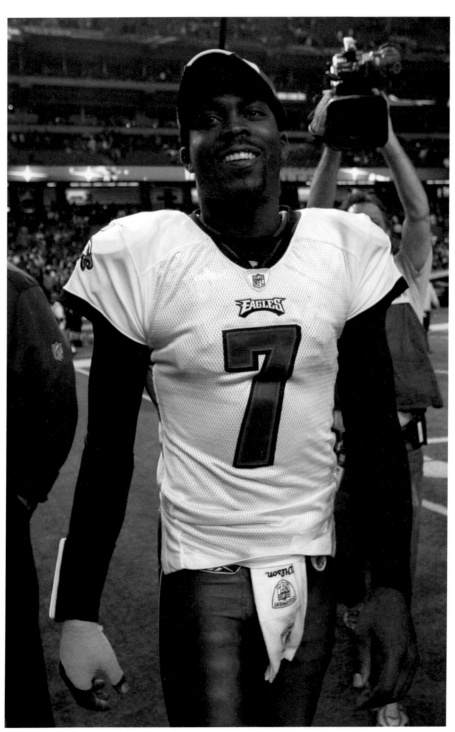

Like Tiger Woods mentioned in the viewpoint, Michael Vick was considered a role model until details of his private life became known.

"We make others our role models. Parents tell their children, 'Be like Tiger. Work hard and practice long hours, and you too might become a champion like he is,'" Kendrick says. "Children also choose their role models apart from their parents' suggestions. They usually choose them because they want to have the lives they lead, do what they do, because they like or admire them or simply because they are famous."

Kendrick agrees with Dr. Bartell that parents would serve their children best by first asking them what they think and feel about what they've heard in the media about Woods. They should then address their children's questions and comments in age-appropriate language, homing in on what seems to be troubling their kids most about the story.

"Parents might do well to prepare themselves to answer difficult questions such as: 'Dad, would you ever do what Tiger did with all those other women?' or 'Mom, would you divorce Dad if he did what Tiger Woods did with those other women?' or 'When his little kids get older and hear or read about what their dad did, how do you think they will feel about their father?'"

EVALUATING THE AUTHORS' ARGUMENTS:

In this viewpoint, Daniel B. Wood acknowledges that millions of people treat Tiger Woods as a role model and assumes that this applies to many other public sports figures as well. The author of the following viewpoint, Armstrong Williams, however, argues that we should not make athletes into role models and heroes. Which view of athletes seems more justified? Support your view with evidence from each viewpoint.

Viewpoint 6

Athletes Should Not Be Considered Role Models

Armstrong Williams

"The real issue is . . . how our society has so conflated celebrity with greatness that we came to view Tiger as a role model to begin with."

Armstrong Williams argues that celebrity athletes have been treated differently from the rest of society from a young age. This upbringing has trained them to believe that they are held to a different and more relaxed standard, so it is not unusual for them to act in ways that do not suit the rest of society. Consequently, it is absurd for society to treat them as heroes, who are those who have demonstrated heroic actions and qualities, such as noble courage. Williams suggests that we turn our attention from celebrities such as sports stars to real heroes.

Armstrong Williams is a contributor to *Human Events* and is a recognized and principled voice for conservative and Christian values.

AS YOU READ, CONSIDER THE FOLLOWING QUESTIONS:

1. According to the author, what are some practices that give the better athletes the idea that they are held to a different standard?
2. What point did Charles Barkley make in 1993 in his Nike commercial?
3. Who are people that we should look to as heroes, according to the author?

For me, it started with Muhammad Ali. I can perfectly recall sitting in the living room with my father, watching as Ali danced around the ring. He moved with a rare mix of fluidity and power, dispatching one rough, plodding opponent after another. He seemed the perfect embodiment of masculine striving. But the best part was after the match had ended. That's when Ali would unleash one of his verbal rants. Full of braggadocio, Ali would proclaim to the world, "I am the greatest." And I believed him. But why? Why was I so willing to listen to Ali? Why do we take any guidance from athletes? In the midst of Tiger Woods' Thanksgiving day car wreck and his apparent infidelity with multiple women, I can't help but wonder why we bother to make heroes of our sportsmen.

After all, everything about the lives of our celebrity athletes encompasses abnormality. From a young age, they are conditioned to believe that they are superior in a Darwinian sense. The moment these physical outliers are spotted on playgrounds, they are courted by "street agents" who fill their heads with dreams of dollars, endorsement deals, celebrity and all those other things that fulfill their adolescent desires to be "feared and worshipped." These promising youths (the fittest, the strongest) are promptly shipped off to shoe-sponsored sports camp where their talents are honed under the adoring gaze of coaches. Money, gifts, promises and special favors from unscrupulous agents, shoe executives and recruiters inevitably follow. And if they hit the big time, their images are beamed across the world with a dreamlike quality based on the persona of the hero.

Along the way, these athletes are sent a message: they—as the fittest—are held to a different standard. They need not worry about finances or academic standards when they have agents and business

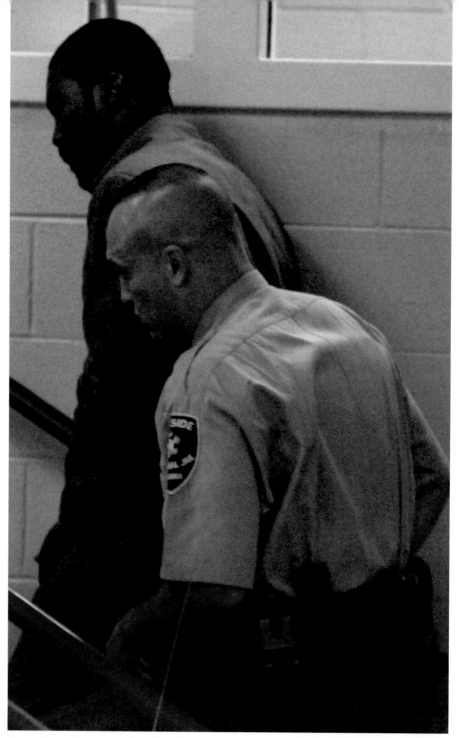

Sports figures lose respect from fans for private misdeeds. In the case of Tiger Woods mentioned in the viewpoint, it was extramarital affairs. In the case of Michael Vick, pictured here, it was his participation in an illegal dog fighting ring for which he spent eighteen months in a federal prison.

executives dying to take care of those things for them. The effect is only to further separate these children from the social conventions that build character in the rest of us.

This kind of emotional coddling can have a disastrous effect. When you have been trained to believe that you are beyond the rules of social decorum, it seems natural to act out your darker impulses. Indulging your personal vanity can be intoxicating. I suspect that Tiger's sexual exploits are fairly representative of how most young men, bombarded with wealth and adulation, would act. It should not be surprising that Tiger gave in to his impulses. In fact, it seems like the most human thing in the world.

I say this not to defend Tiger, but merely to point out the absurdity of expecting our star athletes to behave like heroes. The dictionary tells us that a hero is "a person who, in the opinion of others, has heroic qualities or has performed a heroic act and is regarded as a model or ideal: He was a local hero when he saved the drowning child." What about hitting a golf ball suggests noble courage? Tiger Woods is not a hero. He is a product of pop culture mythology that has become incredibly adept at manufacturing fame.

We live in an era where our star athletes—and our celebrities in general—are treated as our cultural elite. We yearn for a connection to them. It is the height of absurdity that so many people actually feel let down by Tiger's infidelities. Just as it always struck me as bizarre when public [hordes] gather outside the homes of recently deceased celebrities (think Michael Jackson or Princess Diana), sobbing uncontrollably. Somehow, we have come to value our celebrities so much that we feel an actual sense of personal connection to them—even when we've never met them.

The danger is that we have come to admire celebrities more than real heroes. Charles Barkley famously made this point in 1993 when he declared, "a million guys can dunk a basketball in jail; should they be role models?" Later that year, Barkley filmed a self-written Nike commercial in which he argued that athletes should not be considered role models: "I am not a role model," Barkley said. "I am not paid to be a role model. I am paid to wreak havoc on the basketball court. Parents should be role models. Just because I dunk a basketball, doesn't mean I should raise your kids."

Barkley knew as well as anyone that the mere fact of being well known is not enough to transform athletes into moral standard bearers. It is fine to admire athletes for their physical striving. But maybe our admiration should end when they walk off the court. Our children are surrounded by real heroes—our military, law enforcement, teachers, community leaders, and most of all, family members. If we feel a sense of personal betrayal by Tiger's dalliances, perhaps we need to reassess the people we are turning to for moral leadership.

To be sure, Tiger has done a disservice to his family—but only to his family. He does not owe us anything. The real issue is not—as so many people seem to be wondering—whether Tiger Woods can once again be a great role model. It is how our society has so conflated celebrity with greatness that we came to view Tiger as a role model to begin with.

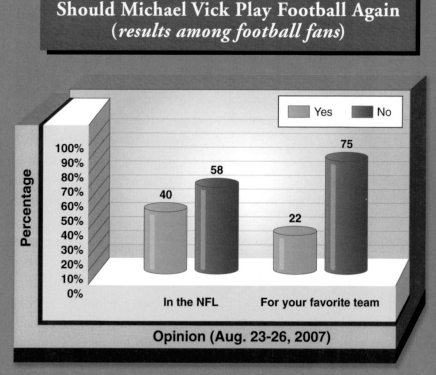

Taken from: Jeffrey M Jones, "Most NFL Fans Say Vick Shouldn't Be Allowed to Play Again," Gallup News Service, August 29, 2007.

In this viewpoint, Armstrong Williams argues that we should not treat athletes as role models and heroes. However, in the previous viewpoint, Daniel B. Wood treats making heroes and role models out of athletes as a natural and everyday occurrence. Which approach to athletes seems more justified? Support your view with evidence from each viewpoint.

Chapter 2

Is Use of Performance-Enhancing Drugs by Athletes a Problem?

The prevalence of performance-enhancing drugs in sports is the number one issue facing sports today.

Baseball's Prohibition on Performance-Enhancing Drugs Is Good Policy

Jim Salisbury

"The game's policy against performance-enhancers is not perfect, but it's working."

In the following viewpoint Jim Salisbury claims that baseball's relatively new policy against performance-enhancing drugs was a positive development. He claims that the policy still has gaps that need to be remedied, but that the policy is working to eliminate the use of performance-enhancing drugs. Salisbury suggests ways to strengthen the policy, including tests for new substances and harsher penalties for violations. He also suggests that players themselves will need to insist on harsher penalties in order to eliminate the current cloud of suspicion surrounding professional baseball players. Salisbury writes about sports for the *Philadelphia Inquirer*.

AS YOU READ, CONSIDER THE FOLLOWING QUESTIONS:
1. According to Salisbury, baseball adopted rules against the use of steroids and other performance-enhancing drugs in what year?
2. The author claims that one of the gaps in baseball's policy against performance-enhancing drugs is the lack of a test for what substance?
3. Salisbury claims that the current suspension for a first-time offense against the policy of performance-enhancing drugs is what?

For many years, Major League Baseball was justifiably criticized for its work (and nonwork) against performance-enhancing drugs.

Just about everyone in and around the sport was either slow to recognize the problem or slow to react to it in the 1990s.

And when baseball and the often uncooperative players' union finally got around to adopting rules against the use of steroids and other performance-enhancers in 2004, the penalties were weak and the system seemed to catch only no-name minor-leaguers and Rafael Palmeiro, a big-league star who thought he was above it all.

Most of the big stars linked to the use of steroids and other performance-enhancers had their names surface outside of MLB's drug dragnet.

Mark McGwire became a white-hot suspect in front of Congress; Barry Bonds through a federal investigation; Roger Clemens through the Mitchell Report; and Alex Rodriguez through a *Sports Illustrated* report.

In recent years, baseball patted itself on the back for toughening its policy (both in testing and penalties), but the names it was snaring were hardly earth-shakers, giving skeptics reason to wonder if the policy really had teeth.

There can be no doubt anymore.

Sure, baseball's drug policy still has holes. (There is still no reliable urine test for human growth hormone; baseball is helping to fund the development of one.) But the sport has proven it will go after the biggest stars in the game if there is reason to believe they are cheating. No one is immune.

That is the biggest thing we learned from the 50-game suspension that Los Angeles Dodgers slugger Manny Ramirez received Thursday.

This wasn't Jordan Schafer, who was an Atlanta Braves minor-leaguer when he received a 50-game suspension for HGH last season. (Schafer has denied using the substance.)

And this wasn't J.C. Romero, a very good major-league reliever but hardly one of the game's biggest names.

This was Manny Ramirez, one of the greatest hitters ever, a member of the 500-homer club, a surefire future Hall of Famer, one of the game's most recognizable players and one of its most highly paid talents.

Like all major-leaguers, Ramirez was tested for performance-enhancers during spring training. His levels for testosterone were unnaturally high and MLB investigators went to work finding out why. Ramirez eventually admitted to using human chorionic gonadotropin (HCG), a fertility drug that increases testosterone production.

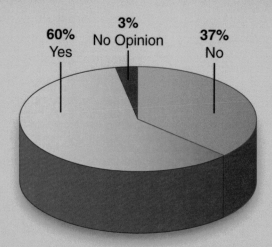

Baseball Fans' Views on Punishment for Steroid Use

Should Players Be Punished?

60%
Yes

3%
No Opinion

37%
No

Taken from: Joseph Carroll, "Baseball Fans: Punish Players Named in Steroid Use Reports," Gallup, December 13, 2007.

Ramirez said he was unaware that HCG was on baseball's list of banned substances. He said a doctor (whom he did not name) prescribed it for a "personal medical issue." He did not say what that issue was, and it's worth noting that he did not seek a therapeutic use exemption from MLB. HCG is considered a performance-enhancing substance. It is often used to kick-start testosterone production that slowed during active steroid use.

Ramirez showed incredible stupidity with this transgression. Why would he jeopardize his legacy by even going near this stuff?

But aside from that, Ramirez's offense showed that despite MLB's beefed-up drug program, players will still take chances and still put banned substances in their bodies to gain an edge. MLB will catch more offenders this season. You can bank on it. And don't be surprised if more big names are caught. If Hall of Fame–caliber talents like Rodriguez and Ramirez are willing to take these risks, you can bet other stars are, too.

Snagging Ramirez shows baseball's drug policy is working, but by the same token, his decision to use a banned performance-enhancer shows that the 50-game suspension for a first-time offense (it's 100 games for a second offense) still isn't harsh enough to get all players' attention.

During spring training, Phillies pitcher Jamie Moyer suggested a one-year suspension for a first positive test and a lifetime ban for a second. Something like this would surely be more of a deterrent to anyone thinking of using performance-enhancers, or should we say cheating? A year is a long time in a sport where players need to keep their edge every day. It would also be a big hit in the wallet. MLB officials and the union need to seriously consider upping the penalty for a first-time offense to a year when the current labor agreement expires after the 2011 season.

The players themselves need to be vocal in pushing for even tougher penalties. That's the thing about this whole sordid era of performance-enhancers: Everyone is a suspect, even the clean guys. But the athletes

Major League Baseball's suspension of future Hall of Famer Manny Ramirez showed that the league will enforce its drug policies and go after big-name players who violate them.

themselves can have an impact in cleaning things up and reducing the cloud of suspicion they live under by speaking up and insisting on the toughest penalties possible.

Sports may never completely rid themselves of performance-enhancers. There will always be some mad scientist out there concocting something new, and some foolish athlete will take it. But efforts to rid the games of these poisons shouldn't just be the responsibility of league officials. The players are the game. If they want a cleaner sport, they can help make it happen.

By all indications, Manny Ramirez had no interest in helping clean up his sport. We know that now. We also know that baseball will go after any drug offender, no matter how big the name. The game's policy against performance-enhancers is not perfect, but it's working.

EVALUATING THE AUTHORS' ARGUMENTS:

In this viewpoint Salisbury contends that the ban on performance-enhancing drugs is a good policy. Why does Steinberg, author of the next viewpoint, disagree with him?

Performance-Enhancing Drugs in Sport Should Not Be Prohibited

Aaron Steinberg

"In short, sports technology isn't just for golf club shafts and running shoes. It's for muscles, ligaments, and organs, and it's getting more sophisticated all the time."

Aaron Steinberg recounts some reasons put forward by former Major League Baseball player José Canseco in his book *Juiced* for using steroids in a controlled way in sports. With largely anecdotal evidence, Canseco mentions the ability of steroids to build stamina and reduce injuries, while offering only low risk to his health. Canseco suggests that the best way to use steroids is with a thorough knowledge of the medication and with frequent consultation with a medical expert. According to Steinberg, Canseco also suggests that steroids are just another tool like meal replacement powders and surgery.

Aaron Steinberg is a writer in Washington, D.C.

AS YOU READ, CONSIDER THE FOLLOWING QUESTIONS:
  1. What did Dayn Perry (a source cited by Steinberg) conclude about the health risks associated with steroid use?
  2. When did Major League Baseball institute league-wide drug testing, and how was that policy revised in 2005?
  3. What is Tommy John surgery and what effect does it have?

On March 17, former baseball star José Canseco told the House Committee on Government Reform exactly what it wanted to hear. The pressure to win, he said, drives pros to steroids and subsequently pushes steroids on kids. "The time has come," he said, "to send a message to America, especially the youth, that these actions, while attractive at first, may tarnish and harm you later."

That isn't exactly the message he sent with his recent pro-steroid tell-all, *Juiced: Wild Times, Rampant 'Roids, Smash Hits, and How Baseball Got Big*. And while his new tune may sound more responsible to legislators' ears, it's actually too bad that the former A's slugger turned his back on his own book. Beyond the typical sports memoir material—Lamborghinis, encounters with Madonna, growing up Latino in baseball—Canseco's book makes a rare and sustained argument in favor of steroids (and substances often used in conjunction with steroids, such as human growth hormone). Coming at a time of full-blown moral panic, with grandstanding senators trampling athletes' privacy rights and the media blaming steroids for everything from brain cancer to suicide, Canseco's position was a welcome one. It's a shame he didn't have the guts to stick with it. . . .

Canseco's lurid anecdotes . . . have helped sell a lot of books, but they've also distracted from his main point. Before the Senate dragged him to Washington and denied him immunity, Canseco didn't think any of the players he'd outed or speculated about should feel the least bit apologetic for using steroids. In his book, though not his testimony, he described steroids as a gift to baseball. Indeed, he wanted to claim credit for bringing them to the league. Whether or not you buy the idea that he's the steroid Prometheus, his book offers good reasons to think baseball should accept the drugs. As he pats himself on the back for nearly 300 pages, he considers two reasonable questions:

1. Just how useful are steroids for baseball players?

2. Can they be used safely?

Most people assume that steroids are only useful for building thick layers of muscle and cranking home runs. As Canseco tells it, though, steroids and human growth hormone can be put to much more sophisticated use. If taken in moderate doses and in certain combinations over a period of time, they can help build strength, quickness, and, most importantly, stamina. The baseball season—a 162-game slog—goes from the beginning of April to the end of September (barring a post-season run). Most players wear out at some point during that period. If a power hitter can use steroids to stay fresh over the course of a season, he could pound out a few extra home runs before October—and that's without any gain in bulk. With millions of dollars at stake, it only makes sense that players would look into this seriously.

The sports press has been quick to diagnose him with steroid-induced fragility, but Canseco insists that steroids helped him cut down

Proponents of performance-enhancing drug use argue that athletes will always be a step ahead of any efforts to test for drug use.

on trips to the disabled list and to recover faster when he was hurt. In his book, Canseco characterizes himself as a scrawny, injury-prone kid who started experimenting with steroids in the minor leagues, just prior to his rapid ascent into the majors. Canseco claims that he began to spike his workouts with liquid testosterone combined with Deca Derbol in 1985. That year he shot from a double-A team in Huntsville, Alabama, to the major leagues. The next season he won Rookie of the Year, and two seasons after that, he was Most Valuable Player. (Canseco's usage then was perfectly legal—Congress did not pass the Anabolic Steroid Control Act until 1990, and Major League Baseball resisted steroid testing until the labor agreement of 2002.)

As far as health risks are concerned, Canseco [admits that steroids reduce the size of the testes but do not adversely affect the function of other private parts]. As with most of the book's assertions, Canseco

Public Perception of Performance-Enhancing Drugs in Baseball

"What percentage of professional baseball players take drugs?"

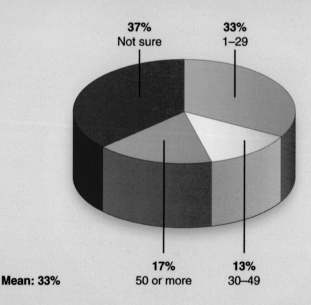

37%
Not sure

33%
1–29

17%
50 or more

13%
30–49

Mean: 33%

Taken from: The Harris Poll #34, May 12, 2004.

makes his case almost entirely with anecdotal evidence. He has plenty of anecdotes to offer, and it isn't easy for the reader to evaluate them. He keeps good company, though. As Dayn Perry has pointed out in these pages (see "Pumped-Up Hysteria," January 2003), most claims about the health effects of steroids and their long-term impact rely heavily on anecdotal evidence and tend to overstate the case. Perry wrote, "A more objective survey of steroids' role in sports shows that their health risks, while real, have been grossly exaggerated . . . and that the worst problems associated with steroids result from their black-market status rather than their inherent qualities."

Juiced doesn't recommend banning steroids. Refreshingly, it doesn't advocate reckless self-medication either. Before using steroids, Canseco counsels, an athlete should learn as much as possible about both the medication and his own body, consult a medical expert regularly, be ready to take training seriously, and probably cut out recreational drugs. In one stand-out passage, Canseco praises the infamous Bay Area Laboratory Co-Operative (BALCO) for its steroid-dispensing ways. "The important thing to know," he writes, "is that, according to the press reports, BALCO was doing it right: They were giving blood tests to [baseball sluggers Barry] Bonds and [Jason] Giambi and the others. As I've been telling people for years, that's the only way to design a cycle that's right for you—to know the details of your body, your different hormone levels, and tailor your dosage accordingly."

Major League Baseball instituted league-wide steroid testing in 2002 as part of a new labor agreement. Under threat of federal legislation, it revisited and expanded that not-yet-expired policy this year. The penalties have been boosted—the leagues will subject players to random testing and to harsher penalties (suspensions, not fines) if caught—and in concert with revised federal law, more substances have been added to the list of the banned. Canseco, largely unconcerned with questions of cheating, argues that steroids are just another example of players taking any competitive advantage they can. He references unsavory baseball aids used through the years—doctored balls, corked bats, amphetamines—and tries to claim them as precursors to steroid use.

It isn't a particularly strong argument, especially for non-players with little sympathy for creative rule-bending to begin with. But he also touches on another, much more convincing argument—not for cheating, but for reconsidering the rule altogether.

Much of the animus toward steroids assumes that they stand apart from all other forms of training—that they are ugly, artificial, and alien to a culture of hard work and honest sweat. But the athlete's project has always been body modification and specialization, and when modern technology impacts elite sports, it doesn't stop at the outer layer of the player's skin. Trying to distinguish natural from artificial methods of training makes less and less sense by the year.

Players hire year-round personal trainers to identify weaknesses in their overall musculature, help build and balance muscle, and hone their reaction times. As recently as the early '80s, weightlifting ballplayers were fairly rare. Now even the sorriest Major League parks have very nice weightlifting facilities and players freely mix weight training with other modern forms of training, such as plyometrics (a form of exercise that concentrates on explosive movements).

The days of rotisserie chicken and beer meals are over, too. Meal replacement powders, multivitamins, and protein bars are the new fuels. Many players even hire private chefs to prepare specialized diets. None of this is done blindly: In order to make sure they get a good return on their diets and training, top athletes may have their blood and urine tested and analyzed regularly. Products such as ZMA (zinc and magnesium) help combat any deficiencies or imbalances. Reportedly, BALCO offered this service to one of their more famous clients, Barry Bonds.

If players don't get the desired performance out of diet, diagnostics, and exercise, there's always surgery. Consider Tommy John surgery, a ligament transplant invented for baseball players and named for the first pitcher to undergo the procedure. It has advanced to the point that the Chicago Cubs' Kerry Wood actually picked up velocity on his pitches after wrecking his arm and having the surgery. In the March 2005 *Wired*, Steven Johnson notes that, "To date, pitchers have opted for the surgery only after suffering ligament damage, but elective-enhancement surgery in baseball is inevitable—and it will show up in lots of other professional sports, too." Johnson also notes that batters hoping to improve their pitch recognition skills can choose another elective procedure: laser eye surgery.

In short, sports technology isn't just for golf club shafts and running shoes. It's for muscles, ligaments, and organs, and it's getting more sophisticated all the time. If such technologies are available to everyone and if the health risks are low—or lower, at least, then getting pulverized by a bulky baserunner sprinting toward home plate—then why single out steroids?

Canseco writes: "These players [who use steroids] may seem like pariahs. But don't be surprised if someday we look back on some of them as pioneers." No one's holding their breath on that one, but it's not as far-fetched as many fans think. And if it does come to pass, Canseco may one day find it convenient to remember that he also wrote, "The performance enhancement that can come with responsible steroid use is nothing to be dismissed . . . it's an opportunity, not a danger." Maybe someone could remind him when this thing blows over.

EVALUATING THE AUTHORS' ARGUMENTS:

In this viewpoint, Aaron Steinberg presents José Canseco's belief that steroids should not be singled out for prohibition out of all the performance-enhancing tools used by athletes. Compare this viewpoint with the previous viewpoint by Jim Salisbury, who praises the Major League Baseball drug testing policy for catching and administering harsh penalties to famous players. Which viewpoint do you agree with more? Support your view with evidence from each viewpoint.

Many Athletes Use Performance-Enhancing Drugs

Steve Weinberg

"Liars abound in Major League Baseball as well as in other professional and amateur sports."

In the following viewpoint Steve Weinberg argues that multiple sources of evidence suggest that the use of performance-enhancing drugs among professional athletes is widespread. He claims that although several baseball players have been singled out in past years for the use of steroids and other substances, many athletes are guilty of using these substances. Weinberg claims that it has been difficult to find the offenders since offending professional athletes have had their identities protected, but recent investigative journalism points to Barry Bonds and other players as having lied to officials about substance use. He concludes that Bonds, along with all the others, should be exposed and punished. Weinberg is a contributor to *The Legal Intelligencer.*

AS YOU READ, CONSIDER THE FOLLOWING QUESTIONS:
1. Weinberg accuses baseball players and others of lying about what?
2. For what reason is Barry Bonds singled out as the primary character using drugs among the athletes named by BALCO, according to the author?
3. According to the author, by 1996 everybody in baseball knew that a lot of players were using what legal substance?

Barry Bonds is a liar. So are other current and past Major League Baseball [MLB] players; at least a few team trainers, coaches, managers and owners; and some executives who run MLB. They all deny that there is widespread use of steroids, human growth hormone and other performance-enhancing substances throughout professional baseball.

Rampant Drug Use Among Athletes

"Lying" is a strong word, an ugly word. But its use seems justified based on evidence presented in *Game of Shadows: Barry Bonds, BALCO and the Steroid Scandal That Rocked Professional Sports*, a book-length exposé by *San Francisco Chronicle* journalists Mark Fainaru-Wada and Lance Williams.

Two other recent books covering many of the same incidents—*Love Me, Hate Me: Barry Bonds and the Making of an Antihero*, by Jeff Pearlman, and *Juicing the Game: Drugs, Power and the Fight for the Soul of Major League Baseball*, by Howard Bryant—bolster the conclusion that liars abound in Major League Baseball as well as in other professional and amateur sports.

When occasional truth-tellers emerge, they end up marginalized. In June 2002, Ken Caminiti revealed in *Sports Illustrated* that he had used steroids in the mid-1990s, which changed him from a player with a medium build into a muscle-bound slugger. He started hitting more home runs and in 1996, while playing for the San Diego Padres, he won the coveted Most Valuable Player award in the National League.

Caminiti said steroid use had become rampant among MLB players. But the baseball establishment, journalists, and fans tended to dismiss him as a washed-up, bitter drug addict. Perhaps in part from the steroid use, Caminiti's health declined and he died in 2004, at age 41. And then last year, former MLB player Jose Canseco created a sensation with his memoir *Juiced: Wild Times, Rampant 'Roids, Smash Hits and How Baseball Got Big.* Critics dismissed him as a greedy author trying to pay off his considerable debts.

Read together, the books relate a morality tale about immensely talented athletes who think only fools refuse to cheat. Why settle for garden-variety greatness, they believe, when sublime greatness can be achieved through amphetamines, human growth hormone, and steroids? The morality tale reaches beyond the professional world to the wider society, as athletes who have not yet graduated from high school decide to fill their still-maturing bodies with performance-enhancing substances—just like their heroes.

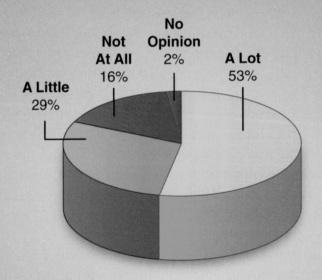

Americans Weigh In on Steroids and Baseball

How much does it matter to you as a baseball fan if professional baseball players use steroids or other performance-enhancing drugs?

No Opinion 2%

Not At All 16%

A Lot 53%

A Little 29%

Taken from: *The New York Times*, March 31, 2008.

Game of Shadows has received the most attention of the three books, partly because it offers access to the normally secret grand jury testimony of Bonds. It also contains the largest amount of information about the multiagency inquiry that spawned the grand jury.

Finding the Offenders

Despite their notable careers, the reporters behind *Game of Shadows* could not have dreamed they would work on a story quite like the steroids exposé. It began with a Sept. 3, 2003, raid by federal agents—propelled by an Internal Revenue Service investigator named Jeff Novitzky—of a nutritional-supplement company founded by Victor Conte and named the Bay Area Laboratory Co-operative, better known as BALCO. When word of the raid reached the *San Francisco Chronicle* newsroom, federal agents would say nothing to the journalists. So editors asked Fainaru-Wada and Williams to investigate. . . .

The reporters produced three scoops in succession: the formation of the grand jury, the subpoena issued to Bonds, and the fact that agents had seized steroids in the BALCO raid. But Fainaru-Wada and Williams still could not name offending athletes in print without airtight confirmation. When then-U.S. Attorney General John Ashcroft indicted Conte for steroid dealing and money laundering, names of specific athletes using the steroids appeared nowhere. Because of their celebrity, the athletes were receiving favorable treatment not usually granted to subjects of grand jury indictments. Eventually, thanks to tireless information gathering, the *San Francisco Chronicle* named seven athletes using performance-enhancing substances supplied by BALCO.

Of the athletes named, Bonds is the primary character, given his single-season home-run record, perhaps the best-known achievement in professional sports history. Bonds had achieved stardom on the baseball field long before hooking up with BALCO. Even with steroids, few humans can hit a 95-mile-an-hour fastball with a thin piece of wood, make a diving catch of a line drive hit to left field, or throw a baseball with enough velocity from left field to prevent a run scoring at home plate.

So although the steroids didn't make Bonds a Major League Baseball player, they perhaps did help him achieve certain athletic goals more readily. Should that mean prosecution within the criminal justice system? Should it mean disciplinary action meted out by MLB? Should it mean invalidation of Bonds' achievements in the record books of the future?

FAST FACT

Barry Bonds left the San Francisco Giants baseball team in 2007, the same year he was indicted for perjury and obstruction of justice regarding the government investigation of BALCO.

In *Love Me, Hate Me*, his biography of Bonds, Jeff Pearlman wrestles with those questions. A former staff writer at *Sports Illustrated* and *Newsday*, Pearlman is a master of on-the-one-hand, on-the-other-hand colloquy. On the one hand, Bonds did not break any MLB rules when he started using steroids in 1998, because the official ban did not occur until five years later. On the other hand, baseball players are not immune from the laws of the United States, and it is against the law to possess and use steroids without documented medical need, as set out in the Controlled Substances Act. . . .

A Widespread Problem

As expansive as Pearlman's book is narrow, *Juicing the Game*, by sports writer Howard Bryant, provides a contrast.

Bryant includes every viewpoint imaginable—those of current players, former players, managers, coaches, trainers, beat journalists, club owners, union representatives, fans, high school teachers, statisticians, legislators, government regulators, and medical researchers. A few have advocated an end to performance-enhancing substances for many years. As for the rest, well, their failures to grapple with the blight of steroids constitute an encyclopedia of denial.

Bryant delves back further than the confessions of Caminiti and Canseco. An especially telling case involves the 1996 season of Brady Anderson, an outfielder for the Baltimore Orioles. By that year, everybody around baseball, including journalists, knew that lots of players were legally ingesting creatine, described by Bryant as "a dietary supplement that had been on the market for years but had been relegated to the fringes of power sports such as weightlifting and football." The

Former baseball home-run king Barry Bonds appears in federal court. He admitted that he lied about steroid use to a grand jury.

substance "enabled an athlete to extend his workout, sometimes by as much as 40 percent beyond his natural limits, and because it allowed a player to work out harder and longer, it also enabled that player to grow stronger."

Before beginning his creatine-fueled workouts, Anderson hit just 10 home runs in his first four MLB seasons. In 1996, he hit 50 home runs. Previously muscular but thin, Anderson started to look like a professional football player. As Bryant makes clear, lots of baseball players began to transform their bodies by breaking the rules. Bonds became the most prominent when he surpassed the single-season home-run record, so it makes sense for the new books to single him out.

If Bonds is punished by Major League Baseball or the federal government, I will be cheering. But my cheers will sound muffled unless the other cheating athletes and their enablers suffer punishment along with Bonds.

EVALUATING THE AUTHORS' ARGUMENTS:

In this viewpoint Weinberg claims that many professional athletes have lied. Who else besides the players would Zirin, author of the next viewpoint, blame for the athletes' lies?

Others Besides Athletes Share the Blame for Use of Performance-Enhancing Drugs

Dave Zirin

"Fault also lies with a system that both elevates and debases sporting superstars, turning them into something not quite human."

In the following viewpoint Dave Zirin argues that professional athletes who are determined to have taken performance-enhancing drugs, as in the case of sprinter Marion Jones, are not entirely to blame. He contends that fault for the use of steroids and other substances is shared by all those who profit from the athlete's success. He scoffs at the idea that people should be outraged by such substance use, claiming that the entire highly profitable sports business is built upon such activity. Zirin is sports editor for the *Nation*. He is the author of *Welcome to the Terrordome: The Pain, Politics, and Promise of Sports, A People's History of Sports in* the United States: 250 Years of Politics, Protest, People, and Play, and What's My Name, Fool? Sports and Resistance in the United States.

AS YOU READ, CONSIDER THE FOLLOWING QUESTIONS:
1. Zirin notes that track and field star Marion Jones returned how many medals after admitting that she took steroids during the 2000 Olympic Games?
2. The author claims that fault for the steroid use of Marion Jones lies with all in "Marion Jones, Inc.," which he claims includes whom?
3. Why does Zirin claim that Marion Jones should be granted amnesty?

When it comes to cynicism, sports fans probably rank somewhere between politicians and mob lawyers. They complain that players are only in sports for the money, that ticket prices amount to robbery and that everybody cheats. And yet, they flock to games, idolize their favorite players and become distraught when their heroes are suddenly revealed to be anything but.

Who Is at Fault?

This contradiction between hardened and hopeful—the desperate desire for role models to emerge from the primordial ooze of sports—explains the widespread dismay at news that track and field heroine Marion Jones had admitted to taking steroids. The one-time icon who graced the covers of both *Sports Illustrated* and *Vogue* admitted to lying to federal prosecutors about her anabolic intake and returned her three gold and two bronze medals earned at the 2000 Sydney Olympic Games. The shock waves following her announcement have been profound, even among the grizzled breed known as sports writers. As Ron Rapoport wrote in the *Los Angeles Times*, Jones, armed with her beauty, skills, and hypnotic smile, "was all but inescapable as the symbol of the possibilities, and the joy, that could flow from a life devoted to sport."

At an October 5 [2007] press conference both tragic and riveting a devastated Jones apologized to her fans through a mask of tears. The looming jail time forced her to speak. Returning her medals was not imposed by the federal government but demanded by United States Anti-Doping Agency.

For Jones, the regret, the public humiliation and the possible time in prison are hers to bear alone. This should not be the case. Fault also lies with a system that both elevates and debases sporting superstars, turning them into something not quite human. Star athletes have become corporations with legs: branded with logos and slogans, and supporting an entire apparatus of advisers and hangers-on. Jones became a one-woman multinational corporation after her 2000 Olympic triumph: the feet of Nike, the face of Oakley Sunglasses, the wrist of TAG Heuer watches.

The Pressure to Take Drugs

All the riches and glory hinged on her ability to shine in Sydney. Jones and her team knew what it would mean if she performed the impossible at the 2000 games and won five gold medals, how it would enshrine her as an immortal of the sport. The tragedy is that even if she hadn't taken steroids, Jones could still have succeeded mightily. Her

"Opening Day," cartoon by Jeff Parker. Copyright © 2009, by Jeff Parker, CagleCartoons.com. All rights reserved.

Marion Jones won five medals at the 2000 Olympic Games. She later had to return them because she had used steroids during the games.

fall should not be hers alone. It's an indictment of every "employee" of Marion Jones, Inc., every Olympic overseer who basked in her glory, every corporate sponsor who made her its brand. As steroids entered her orbit and the federal government loomed, they reacted with either benign neglect or malignant intent. They all deserve to shoulder some of this weight.

In a world in which the possibility of escaping poverty—whether it's baseball in the Dominican Republic, basketball in Eastern Europe or football in the Florida Panhandle—is a major motive for many athletes to turn professional, the drive to succeed is rarely fraught with moral conundrums. Success means money, not only for you but also for the "employees" of you, the corporation. You win or everyone loses. As Ricky Bobby says in the film *Talladega Nights*, "If you ain't first, you're last."

A multibillion-dollar sports empire has been built on this ethically flimsy foundation, creating unexpected platforms for sanctimony from the likes of Peter Ueberroth, the chairman of the US Olympic Committee, who demanded that Jones return her medals.

But what keeps the Ueberroths, the Bud Seligs [baseball commissioner] up at night is the thought that it is all built on a house of anabolic cards: on the ability of athletes to evolve on fast-forward and continue their ability to amaze. As a baseball player once told me, the problem with the debate on performance-enhancing drugs is that "punishment is an individual issue but distribution is a team issue."

A Systemic Failure

Marion Jones should not spend one minute in prison for lying to the feds, and that's not just because President [George W.] Bush and [assistant to President Bush] Scooter Libby have given us precedent to believe that such punishments might be "unduly harsh." She was lying to protect Marion Jones, Inc. She was lying to protect Ueberroth's

Olympic ideal, which in the twenty-first century has become little more than a frenzy of greed and graft in pursuit of gold.

Marion Jones should be granted amnesty on the grounds that the entire system sets athletes up for failure. As fans and followers of sport, it's time to drop the Pollyanna act and the hero worship. It's time to stop demanding the super human and start letting the guardians of sport know that anyone who benefits from an athlete's rise to the top should also accompany their fall from grace.

EVALUATING THE AUTHORS' ARGUMENTS:

In this viewpoint Zirin argues that Marion Jones should be granted amnesty for her use of performance-enhancing drugs. What authors in this chapter would disagree with Zirin? Explain your answer.

Congress Is Right to Investigate the Use of Steroids in Baseball

Robert Housman

"If federal intervention is needed to get the job done, so be it."

In the following viewpoint Robert Housman argues that intervention by Congress and the federal government into performance-enhancing drug use in sports is warranted. Housman gives four reasons why government intervention is warranted, citing legal reasons, moral reasons, the similarity of sports to other government-regulated business, and the ability of government to effectively regulate drug use in sports. Housman is a partner at BookHill Partners in Washington, D.C., and from 1997 to 2001 served as assistant director for strategic planning in the White House Office of National Drug Control Policy (ONDCP). He is the former deputy head of the U.S. delegation to the World Anti-Doping Agency (WADA).

AS YOU READ, CONSIDER THE FOLLOWING QUESTIONS:
1. In what way is athlete use of performance-enhancing drugs a legal issue, according to Housman?
2. What does Housman identify as one example of a federal benefit under the law given to sports leagues?
3. What agency does the author suggest could be turning into a quasi-governmental oversight body to combat drug use in sports?

When the House Government Reform Committee recently called baseball stars and league officials to testify about steroid use, critics complained that Congress and the federal government should not get involved in sports, even regarding drug use. These critics were off the mark.

First, the federal government already has a role in this issue. It is a federal crime to possess and distribute steroids and certain other performance-enhancing drugs. In fact, one reason baseball now faces a steroid crisis is that federal authorities have only recently begun seriously addressing their responsibility to crack down on illegal steroids.

The Clinton administration drug czar's office, which then headed efforts to address drug use in sports, had to cajole the Drug Enforcement Administration to increase enforcement against steroids and related drugs. As a result, steroids are widely available to both big leaguers and little leaguers.

Second, the federal government already has a moral and statutory responsibility to educate young people about the dangers of illegal drug use, including steroids.

Performance-enhancing drugs seriously risk the health and safety of users, especially young people. The risks of steroid use include: elevated cholesterol levels, increased incidence of heart disease, addiction, serious liver damage, sex-trait changes and often severe behavioral changes, particularly heightened aggressiveness. No victory is worth the damage these substances do to a person—just ask the parents who told the hearing their children committed suicide because of steroid use. Stars who use these dangerous drugs set a deadly example for children. The administration and Congress have a role in making athletes, parents, children, coaches and others aware of risks.

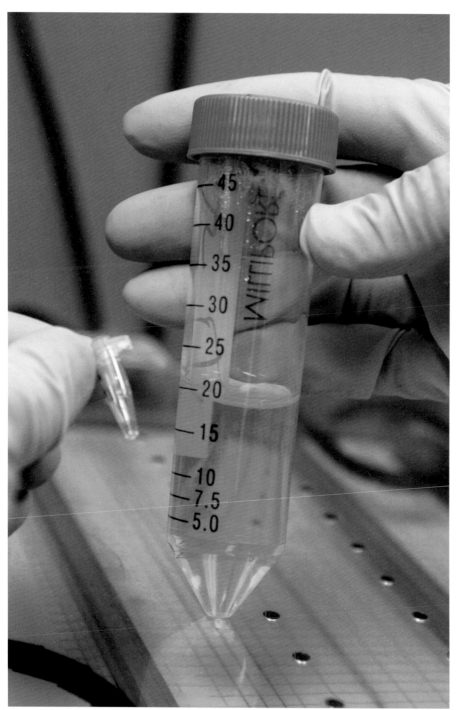

The U.S. Anti-Doping Agency's UCLA laboratory tests over forty thousand urine samples a year from Olympic athletes, professional football players, and minor league baseball players.

Is Use of Performance-Enhancing Drugs by Athletes a Problem? 73

Third, critics of federal involvement erroneously portray sports as somehow different. In fact, sports, especially Major League Baseball and the other pro leagues, are big businesses.

Great plays and devoted fans notwithstanding, the pro leagues involve companies and individuals overwhelmingly in it for the money—and there is nothing wrong with that. For those who doubt sports are basically about money, consider the long list of teams, from baseball's old Washington Senators to the NFL's Baltimore Colts, that were simply moved away from their adoring fans when they fell on fiscal hard times.

In business terms, use of steroids has essentially cooked the record-books of these companies. If such fraud and abuse occurred in any other market sector, there would be no question federal involvement is appropriate. There should be none here. Moreover, the sports leagues enjoy substantial federal benefits under law, including a vital antitrust exemption. In the other sectors, such as broadcasting, where special privileges are granted by the federal government, companies are subject to public responsibilities and federal oversight.

FAST FACT

A congressional hearing was held regarding Major League Baseball in March 2005, interviewing several players and baseball executives about steroid use.

Fourth, some critics have the simply wrongheaded idea that the unique nature of sports makes impossible a positive federal role in fixing this problem. Overwhelmingly in other nations, professional sports leagues are subject to independent drug testing and enforcement agencies that are, one way or another, governmental or quasi-governmental bodies. For example, sports-crazed Australia operates the Australian Sports Drug Agency, one of the world's finest programs.

In fact, the director of the Clinton White House office on drug control policy, Gen. Barry McCaffrey, played a critical role in setting up just such a body for the U.S. Olympic athletes.

The U.S. Anti-Doping Agency, or USADA, has made tremendous strides in safeguarding America's Olympic athletes. The USADA could easily be expanded into a quasi-governmental oversight body responsible for counterdrug programs for the pro leagues as well as the Olympic and elite amateur ranks.

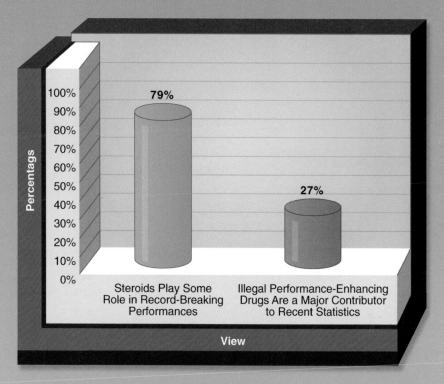

Baseball Players' Views on Steroids and Other Drugs

79% — Steroids Play Some Role in Record-Breaking Performances

27% — Illegal Performance-Enhancing Drugs Are a Major Contributor to Recent Statistics

Percentags

View

Taken from: Chris Jenkins, "Players Admit Steroids Changed Baseball," USA Today, March 15, 2005.

No antidrug program, whether run by the leagues or by the federal government, will be perfect. There is a constant struggle between those who want to protect the ideal of sports and the dreams of clean athletes and those who will go to any length, including using drugs, to win.

However, there is no question current anti-doping programs are woefully inadequate. The leagues and players have had countless chances to fix this problem. If federal intervention is needed to get the job done, so be it.

In fact, given the problems professional baseball faces in this scandal, the league might well consider federal help as something like a relief pitcher coming in late in the game to rescue it from a very costly loss.

EVALUATING THE AUTHORS' ARGUMENTS:

In this viewpoint Housman argues that congressional intervention into the issue of steroids in professional sports is warranted. Why does the *Gazette*, author of the next viewpoint, disagree with this?

Congress Is Wrong to Investigate the Use of Steroids in Baseball

Colorado Springs (CO) *Gazette*

> "It's not the job of Congress to burnish the reputation of a private sports league."

In the following viewpoint the *Colorado Springs* (CO) *Gazette* argues that Congress has no business investigating the use of steroids in Major League Baseball. The *Gazette* contends that the link between the federal government and baseball is weak and that government intervention is not warranted. The authors suggest that it is the job of fans to express their opinion about the use of performance-enhancing drugs and that this does not require Congress to take action. The *Gazette* concludes that the general public needs to be more realistic about the reality of professional sports and athletes and take athletes off the pedestal that they have placed them on. The *Gazette* is a newspaper in Colorado Springs, Colorado.

Pumped-up on its own particular kind of "juice"—arguably the most dangerous drug of all: power—Congress this week muscles its way into a controversy in which it doesn't belong; namely, alleged steroid use by professional baseball players. The House Government Reform Committee, which formerly confined itself to trying to combat waste, mismanagement and abuse in the federal government, evidently has been so successful at making the federal government a model of efficiency that it now has the time to take on other tasks—such as cleaning up Major League Baseball and lecturing young people about the dangers and illegality of using performance-enhancing drugs. If the committee cleans up baseball as effectively as it has reformed the federal government, heaven help baseball.

The committee has issued subpoenas demanding the appearance of a number of players and major league executives at Thursday's hearing, including stars present and past such as Mark McGwire, Sammy Sosa, Jason Giambi, Curt Schilling, Rafael Palmeiro, Frank Thomas and Jose Canseco. Some of the players are balking at the invitation, as well they should. Canseco will be there, because he's got a tell-all book to hawk. But what does any of this have to do with reforming government?

The only link between major league baseball and the federal government that we can find is that the former is granted an anti-trust exemption by the latter, and thus has some leverage it should probably relinquish anyway. This clearly is nothing more, therefore, than an opportunity for a few members of Congress to preen in the spotlight.

Under political pressure, major league baseball and its players union agreed in January to a steroids-testing policy. Pressure from Congress and Arizona's Sen. John McCain were largely responsible for this.

In February 2008 the House Government Reform Committee held hearings on the use of illegal performance-enhancing drugs in Major League Baseball.

Baseball owners saw an unspoken either-or coming out of Washington—if you like your antitrust exemption, you'll do this—and acted accordingly. Players, too, saw fans becoming more suspicious that some of the record-breaking performances of the last decade or so were artificially induced.

In our opinion, eliminating steroid use from the game is a matter best resolved between the league, team owners and the players, in response to a signal of disapproval from fans. But we see little of the latter. All but the very naive already guessed that something other than eating Wheaties accounts for the enhanced size, speed and performance of many pro athletes. And few people any longer equate athletic performance with moral virtue.

Those fans who disapprove of the drug trend, or the league's response to it, can express that disapproval by staying away from the games and television sets. Any league that wants to prevent the loss of those kind of fans will respond accordingly. Those fans who couldn't care less, and are more than happy to watch chemically engineered behemoths smashing baseballs over the center-field fence, will continue to support the sport, if there are enough of them to do so. The market, in other words, will sort the matter out satisfactorily, without Congress' intervention.

FAST FACT

In 2007 former U.S. senator George J. Mitchell submitted a report revealing the results of an investigation into the use of performance-enhancing drugs in Major League Baseball, resulting in further congressional hearings in 2008.

And as for America's impressionable youth, whom Congress fears might be corrupted if baseball and professional sports are tainted by the scandal? We live in troubled times, indeed, if parents still are holding up professional sports stars as role models for their kids. It's time they instead tell young people the truth—that sports stars are no different from other mortals. Some are worthy of respect, others aren't; some play fair, others cheat; some deserve to be cheered, others jeered. It's not the job of Congress to burnish the reputation of a private sports league, or to immerse young Americans in a warm and fuzzy sports fantasy bubble bath.

But Congress doesn't see it that way. "House rules give this committee the authority to investigate any matter at any time, and we are authorized to request or compel testimony and document production related to any investigation," one committee staffer explained. In other words, Congress is doing it because Congress can do it.

It seems that professional athletes aren't the only people whose insatiable desire for more power leads them to extremes.

Sunshine Week Highlights Public's Right to Know

Few things are as critical for the proper functioning of a free and democratic society as transparent government. People must be able to know what their leaders are doing, how their resources are being utilized and what government officials are doing behind closed doors. For this reason, media organizations across the country have created a nationwide campaign to press for better public access to government information, and greater awareness of freedom of information issues. This week, Sunshine Week, this newspaper and other media outlets will focus on issues regarding public access to government's inner workings.

As might be expected, many officials chafe at the constant pressure to maintain open government and have a tendency to want to control the flow of information, especially the embarrassing, controversial or illegal kind. But much is riding on the public's right to know, not just the good, but the bad and the ugly as well.

Government has only gotten more closed since Sept. 11, 2001. "The trend toward secrecy is unmistakable," Associated Press President Tom Curley stated this year, when Sunshine Week was announced. Whether because of bureaucratic inertia or a desire to avoid scrutiny, too much secrecy can result not just in a waste of taxpayer money, but in a threat to public safety. So this week, think about why the government likes to keep you in the dark, and join us in reminding government officials of the public's right to know.

EVALUATING THE AUTHORS' ARGUMENTS:

In this viewpoint the *Gazette* claims that fans should be the ones to express approval or disapproval about performance-enhancing drugs. Given this, do you think they would be more likely to agree with Salisbury or Steinberg—previous authors in this chapter—about having a policy against such drugs?

Chapter 3

Should College Sports Be Reformed?

College football today is a multibillion-dollar industry for the National Collegiate Athletic Association, and some say reform is needed.

College Athletes Should Be Paid

Michael Lewis

> *"Everyone associated with [college football] is getting rich except the people whose labor creates the value."*

In the following viewpoint Michael Lewis argues that college football players should be paid. He claims that college football is a huge moneymaker for universities, yet the policy of not paying student players is supposedly based on the idea that college sports are not about money. Lewis decries the assertion made by colleges that the primary goal for college athletes is to get an education. He proposes that college football be structured much like professional football, with players taking their share of the profits. Lewis is a financial journalist, a *Vanity Fair* contributing editor, and author of *The Blind Side: Evolution of a Game*.

AS YOU READ, CONSIDER THE FOLLOWING QUESTIONS:
1. Lewis claims that several dozen college football coaches now make over how much a year?
2. What does the author say is the principle behind the National Collegiate Athletic Association policy of not paying college football players?
3. According to the author, in 2005 the football teams in Division 1-A generated how much money for their colleges?

The three most lucrative college football teams in 2005—Notre Dame, Ohio State and the University of Texas—each generated more than $60 million for their institutions. That number, which comes from the Department of Education, fails to account for the millions of dollars alumni donated to their alma maters because they were so proud of their football teams. But it still helps to explain why so many strangers to football success have reinvented themselves as football powerhouses (Rutgers?), and also why universities are spending huge sums on new football practice facilities, new football stadium skyboxes and new football coaches.

College Football and Money

Back in 1958 the University of Alabama lured Bear Bryant with a promise of $18,000 a year, or the rough equivalent of $130,000 today; last year the university handed Nick Saban an eight-year deal worth roughly $32 million. Several dozen college football coaches now earn more than $1 million a year—and that's before the books, speeches, endorsement deals and who knows what else. Earlier this season the head coach at Texas A&M, Dennis Franchione, was caught topping up his $2.09 million salary by selling to Aggie alums, for $1,200 a pop, his private football-gossip newsletter.

The sports media treated that particular scheme as scandalous. Texas A&M made its coach apologize, and promise to stop writing for a living. But really Dennis Franchione's foray into high-priced journalism was just an ingenious extension of the entrepreneurial spirit that's turned college football into a gold mine. The scandal wasn't what he did but how it was made to seem—unusually greedy.

College football's best trick play is its pretense that it has nothing to do with money, that it's simply an extension of the university's mission to educate its students. Were the public to view college football as mainly a business, it might start asking questions. For instance: why are these enterprises that have nothing to do with education and everything to do with profits exempt from paying taxes? Or why don't they pay their employees?

The Commercialization of College Sports

This is maybe the oddest aspect of the college football business. Everyone associated with it is getting rich except the people whose labor creates the value. At this moment there are thousands of big-time college football players, many of whom are black and poor. They perform for

Top Ten Most Valuable College Football Teams in 2007

South Bend, IN	Knoxville, TN	Ann Arbor, MI	Columbus, OH
University of Notre Dame $101 million	University of Tennessee $74 million	University of Michigan $85 million	Ohio State University $71 million

Austin, TX
University of Texas $92 million

Baton Rouge, LA	Birmingham, AL	Athens, GA
Louisiana State University $76 million	University of Alabama $72 million	University of Georgia $90 million

Auburn, AL	Gainesville, FL
Auburn University $73 million	University of Florida $84 million

the intense pleasure of millions of rabid college football fans, many of whom are rich and white. The world's most enthusiastic racially integrated marketplace is waiting to happen.

But between buyer and seller sits the National Collegiate Athletic Association [N.C.A.A.], to ensure that the universities it polices keep all the money for themselves—to make sure that the rich white folk do not slip so much as a free chicken sandwich under the table to the poor black kids. The poor black kids put up with it because they find it all but impossible to pursue N.F.L. [National Football League] careers unless they play at least three years in college. Less than one percent actually sign professional football contracts and, of those, an infinitesimal fraction ever make serious money. But their hope is eternal, and their ignorance exploitable.

Put that way the arrangement sounds like simple theft; but up close, inside the university, it apparently feels like high principle. That principle, as stated by the N.C.A.A., is that college sports should never be commercialized. But it's too late for that. College football already is commercialized, for everyone except the people who play it. Were they businesses, several dozen of America's best-known universities would be snapped up by private equity tycoons, who would spin off just about everything but the football team. (The fraternities they might keep.)

If the N.C.A.A. genuinely wanted to take the money out of college football it'd make the tickets free and broadcast the games on public television and set limits on how much universities could pay head coaches. But the N.C.A.A. confines its anti-market strictures to the players—and God help the interior lineman who is caught breaking them. Each year some player who grew up with nothing is tempted by a booster's offer of a car, or some cash, and is never heard from again.

The Lie About College Football

The lie at the bottom of the fantasy goes something like this: serious college football players go to college for some reason other than to play football. These marvelous athletes who take the field on Saturdays and generate millions for their colleges are students first, and football players second. They are like Franciscan monks set down in the gold mine. Yes, they play football, but they have no interest in the money. What they're really living for is that degree in criminology.

Of course, no honest person who has glimpsed the inside of a big-time college football program could actually believe this. Even from the outside the college end of things seems suspiciously secondary. If serious college football players are students first, why—even after a huge N.C.A.A. push to raise their graduation rates—do they so alarmingly fail to graduate? Why must the N.C.A.A. create incentives for football coaches to encourage their players even to attend classes? Why do we never hear of a great high school football player choosing a college for the quality of its professors? Why, when college football coaches sell their programs to high school studs, do they stress the smoothness of the path they offer to the N.F.L.?

It's not that football players are too stupid to learn. It's that they're too busy. Unlike the other student on campus, they have full-time

Football coaches Mack Brown of the University of Texas, left, and Nick Saban of the University of Alabama, both head programs that generate millions of dollars in revenue for their schools. Critics say some of that revenue should be shared with players.

jobs: playing football for nothing. Neglect the task at hand, and they may never get a chance to play football for money.

Pay for Players

Last year the average N.F.L. team had revenue of about $200 million and ran payrolls of roughly $130 million: 60 percent to 70 percent of a team's revenues, therefore, go directly to the players. There's no reason those numbers would be any lower on a college football team—and there's some reason to think they'd be higher. It's easy to imagine the Universities of Alabama ($44 million in revenue), Michigan ($50 million), Georgia ($59 million) and many others paying the players even more than they take in directly from their football operations, just to keep school spirit flowing. (Go Dawgs!)

But let's keep it conservative. In 2005, the 121 Division 1-A football teams generated $1.8 billion for their colleges. If the colleges paid out 65 percent of their revenues to the players, the annual college football payroll would come to $1.17 billion. A college football team has 85 scholarship players while an N.F.L. roster has only 53, and so the money might be distributed a bit differently.

"You'd pay up for the most critical positions," one N.F.L. front-office executive told me on the condition that I not use his name. "You'd pay more for quarterbacks and left tackles and pass rushing defensive ends. You'd pay less for linebackers because you'd have so many of them. You could just rotate them in and out."

FAST FACT

According to Forbes magazine, in 2009 University of Southern California's football coach Pete Carroll had a salary of $4.4 million a year.

A star quarterback, he thought, might command as much as 8 percent of his college team's revenues. For instance, in 2005 the Texas Longhorns would have paid Vince Young roughly $5 million for the season. In quarterbacking the Longhorns free of charge, Young, in effect, was making a donation to the university of $5 million a year—and also, by putting his health on the line, taking a huge career risk.

Perhaps he would have made this great gift on his own. The point is that Vince Young, as the creator of the economic value, should have had the power to choose what to do with it. Once the market is up and running players who want to go to enjoy the pure amateur experience can continue to play for free.

And you never know. The N.C.A.A. might one day be able to run an honest advertisement for the football-playing student-athlete: a young man who valued so highly what the University of Florida had to teach him about hospitality management that he ignored the money being thrown at him by Florida State.

EVALUATING THE AUTHORS' ARGUMENTS:

In this viewpoint Lewis suggests that college athletes are exploited under the current model. Does Sack, author of the next viewpoint, agree or disagree with this claim? Explain your answer.

College Athletes Should Not Be Paid

Allen Sack

> *"One can only hope that the NCAA will abandon its present course toward building a sports entertainment empire and consider a return to bona-fide amateurism."*

In the following viewpoint Allen Sack contends that college athletes should not be paid. He claims that college sports have moved from a model of amateurism toward the model of professionalism. Because of this greater professionalism, Sack claims that certain college athletes should have access to increased rights and benefits. He concludes that the only way to fairly deny college athletes some perks is to return to a genuine model of amateurism in college sports. Sack is a professor at the University of New Haven and played on Notre Dame's 1966 national championship football team. He is the author of *Counterfeit Amateurism: An Athlete's Journey Through the Sixties to the Age of Academic Capitalism.*

AS YOU READ, CONSIDER THE FOLLOWING QUESTIONS:
1. According to Sack, what year did the National Collegiate Athletic Association begin to allow athletic scholarships?
2. What kinds of rights and benefits does the author claim should be given to college athletes who are recruited and subsidized?
3. What does Sack think college athletes are going to do in the coming decade?

As the NCAA's season-ending basketball tournament approaches, talk of the future of college sports is hot. One of the most controversial questions: Should the college athletes who are the main attraction at this multibillion dollar March Madness tournament be paid? As a longtime supporter of amateur sport, my answer is no. The amateur model embraced by the founding fathers of the National Collegiate Athletic Association (NCAA) in 1905 remains the best fit for the academic mission of higher education.

However, if the NCAA doesn't change the status quo—which is on a fast course toward building a sports entertainment empire—how could they *not* pay athletes or at least extend worker's rights?

From Amateurism Toward Professionalism

There would be good reasons for supporting the prohibition against paying college athletes *if* the NCAA's claim were true that big-time college athletes—like those who will electrify the crowds at this year's Final Four—are merely "amateurs" engaged in sport during their free time. That claim, though, has absolutely no support in recent history, aside from some Division III exceptions.

When I played football for Notre Dame in the 1960s, the NCAA had already compromised its half-century commitment to amateur principles. In 1957, after years of intense internal debate, the NCAA caved under pressure to subsidize athletes, and voted to allow athletic scholarships. It was at this point that commercialized college sports started down the slippery slope toward open professionalism.

At first, NCAA rules allowed these scholarships to be awarded for four years, as I was assured mine would be when I was recruited in the 1960s—regardless of my performance on the athletic field. Unfortunately, since

I graduated, scholarships have taken on the trappings of an employment contract.

At the height of student revolts on college campuses in 1967, the association adopted rules that allowed the immediate termination of scholarship aid to athletes who challenge the authority of a coach or withdraw from sports voluntarily. In 1973, four-year scholarships were relegated to the scrap heap. Today, scholarships are awarded on a year-to-year basis. Athletes who have been injured or who turn out to be recruiting mistakes can be fired.

The Rights of College Athletes

During the past four decades, the NCAA has crafted a payment system that provides a relatively cheap and steady supply of blue-chip

The NCAA Men's Basketball Tournament's Final Four generates millions of dollars for the participating schools. Many feel the NCAA needs to reform its version of "amateur" sports and address the needs of student athletes.

athletes for the burgeoning business of collegiate sports and gives coaches the kind of control over them that employers have over employees. It is little wonder that a recent survey of college athletes by the NCAA found that the majority of those polled identify themselves more as athletes than as students.

At schools that award no athletic scholarships, such as those in the Ivy League or the NCAA's Division III, athletes are students first, and even though athletes get a break in admissions, scandals like those that plague big-time college sports are rare.

However, athletes who are recruited and subsidized to provide commercial entertainment for millions of Americans are a very different matter. Because they are already essentially paid to play, they deserve the same rights and benefits as other employees, including medical benefits, workers' compensation when injured, and the right

to use their God-given talents to build some financial security for their families while still in college. The denial of these rights is morally unconscionable.

Two Options for College Sports

At present, a fairly small number of athletes, many of them African-American football and basketball players, produce much of the revenue that keeps entire athletic programs afloat. Because most athletic programs run deficits, paying these athletes a salary of some kind would be a stretch. At the very least, however, the athletes who put fans in the seats and in front of TV sets deserve a genuine opportunity to receive the education they were promised and a stipend to cover the full cost of their education.

These athletes also need players' associations to bargain for better medical benefits and the right to engage in the same kinds of entrepreneurial ventures that are the stock and trade of celebrity coaches.

Scholarship athletes should be able to endorse products, accept pay for speaking engagements, and get a cut of the profits universities make by marketing their images. They should also be allowed to have agents to help them plan their financial futures.

In past decades, the NCAA substituted a counterfeit version of amateurism for the real thing. It happened so slowly that most people did not notice. As college sports moves into the second decade of the new millennium, athletes will undoubtedly organize to demand a bigger share of the money. When this occurs, one can only hope that the NCAA will abandon its present course toward building a sports entertainment empire and consider a return to bona-fide amateurism.

EVALUATING THE AUTHORS' ARGUMENTS:

In this viewpoint Sack laments the move away from amateurism within college sports. Do you think that the author of the previous viewpoint, Lewis, would agree with Sack that a return to amateurism is the most preferable model for college sports? Why or why not?

College Athletics Should Be Privatized So Universities Can Focus on Academics

Silvio Laccetti

"State U should consider privatizing big-time college sports programs."

In the following viewpoint Silvio Laccetti contends that big-time college sports should be privatized—separated from the university's academic program. Laccetti claims that recent research showing gaps between athletes' admissions scores and non-athletes' scores proves that the recruitment of athletes is lowering academic standards. He concludes that the big sports programs should be separated from academics and run as private companies, paying their employees, who would no longer be students. Laccetti is a columnist and professor of social sciences at Stevens Institute of Technology in New Jersey.

AS YOU READ, CONSIDER THE FOLLOWING QUESTIONS:
1. According to the author, which college had the highest average SAT score for basketball players?
2. Laccetti suggests that privatized college sports teams could be funded by a coalition of what three entities?
3. The author proposes that athletes in a newly privatized college sports program could play as paid employees for how many years?

A cademics or athletics? That is the historic question big-time state universities must address.

Athletes are exploited, admission standards corrupted and taxpayer resources diverted. The NCAA [National Collegiate Athletic Association] plays catch-up with its regulations while recently giving an OK for colleges to contact prospects in grammar school! The general public seems to expect entertainment rather than education from its biggest colleges.

Athletic Admissions Standards

The most recent comprehensive investigation of State U athletics versus academics was published at the end of December 2008 in the *Atlanta Journal-Constitution.*

Journalist Mike Knobler analyzed data, as reported in the NCAA Certification Self-Study, from the top 54 U.S. college athletic programs. His general findings show: "Nationwide, football players average 220 and basketball players 227 points lower on the SAT than do their classmates."

Special admissions percentages for athletes on scholarship are many times higher than for the rest of the student body. At schools like Rutgers, UCLA [University of California at Los Angeles] and LSU [Louisiana State University] they accounted for more than one-half of the athletic scholarships.

Oklahoma University and the University of Florida—participants in this year's [2009] football championship game—ranked 42nd and 50th in football SATs. Nationally, in the group of 54, the highest football SAT was Georgia Tech, at 1,028 and the highest basketball SAT belonged to Iowa State, with 1,087. OSU [Oklahoma State University] and Louisville tied for lowest football SATs at 878 and Texas ranked last with 797 for basketball SATs—all SAT score averages.

Can admissions standards for these athletes get any lower?

This is the big college equivalent of "pay to play." To be competitive, they have to accept the most marginal players.

Two Approaches

Of interest to Buffalo area readers is a comparison of the University at Buffalo [UB] to Rutgers. Both schools have committed to upgrading athletics to big-time status, but there are vast differences in approaches.

Rutgers, the State University of New Jersey, may well be the poster child for university problems with big-time athletics. The school committed to a top 20 football program for the 21st century. But in the rush to athletic glory, many irregularities and problems arose: a questionable stadium expansion may need new taxpayer funds to complete; there were "secret" compensation packages for the coach, which caused a furor when revealed; and to save money, six Olympic sports were eliminated.

At Rutgers University a rush to achieve top 20 football revenue became a scandal when athletic director Robert E. Mulcahy, center with tie, resigned because of irregularities and problems arising from a multibillion-dollar stadium expansion.

UB has taken a more cautious and orderly approach. Athletic administrators have committed to bringing high-quality athletics and academic contributors to campus. According to UB's Stephen Marth, sports editor of the student newspaper, student interest is very high and the campus has been energized by recent athletic successes.

A comparison of UB to Rutgers and Syracuse is worthwhile:

- Average SAT of all students: UB, 1,199; Rutgers, 1,184; Syracuse, 1,185.
- Average SAT of scholarship players in football: UB, 996; Rutgers, 938; Syracuse, 922.
- Average SAT of scholarship players in basketball: UB, 1,004; Rutgers, 859; Syracuse, 858.

UB basketball shows much superior scores in the comparison and to the whole sample of 54. But scores for football follow the national pattern.

Privatize College Sports

So what could be done then? State U should consider privatizing big-time college sports programs. Don't expect a business plan in a 750-word column, but here are some salient points.

Detach big-time athletics from their colleges. Operate State U football and basketball through an independent private corporation, which will give the university a generous cut of the profits. Created through private capitalization, these new companies could be funded by a coalition of private boosters, alumni and regional businesses. They would be managed like any other business. Corporate Stock could be issued and traded.

Privatization is not disruptive. Leagues can remain the same, as well as names and game sites. Most personnel will remain the same, with checks on excessive compensation. A special benefit in this scenario is the opportunity for minority participation and ownership in these new corporations.

Pay the performers. Athletes would participate on these teams for three years, ages 18 to 20, as paid employees. As in the European system, only the best would rise from the ranks of college to the professional system. If a player doesn't make the professional grade, that individual can then start higher education to prepare for a new career.

College Football SAT Scores

The Top 10

School	Average
Georgia Tech	1028
Oregon State	997
Michigan	997
Virginia	993
Purdue	974
Indiana	973
Hawaii	968
California	967
Colorado	966
Iowa	964

The Bottom 10

School	Average
Oklahoma State	878
Louisville	878
Memphis	890
Florida	890
Texas Tech	901
Arkansas	910
Texas A&M	911
Mississippi State	911
Washington State	916
Michigan State	917

Taken from: Mike Knobler, "College Athletes: Academic Performance Behind the Line on Grades," *Atlanta Journal Constitution*, December 28, 2008.

While employed, these athletes would receive leadership training in business and communications skills, via the common practice of in-house corporate training. Hopefully great numbers of them would find careers in college sports corporations or in the various allied companies and media that work with State U. (Degree not required.)

Several major advantages result. State U makes a profit from its contracts. It no longer pours scarce resources into athletics instead of academics. The problem of exploited or unqualified student athletes disappears.

Football and basketball would continue to be varsity sports in State U, but modeled on Division 3 or European University sports. There would still be all the competition, good fun and development of life skills for participants, with a degree of fan interest.

Plans to place education ahead of big-time athletics will surely cause the sparks to fly. Old historical patterns die hard. Entrenched interests retrench. But after the sparks fly and there is change, then universities can focus on a different contest—keeping America competitive in the world.

EVALUATING THE AUTHORS' ARGUMENTS:

In this viewpoint Laccetti claims that college athletics should be privatized to avoid sacrificing academic rigor in the admission of athletes. How does Harlin's position, in the next viewpoint, differ from Laccetti's? Are there any points upon which they both agree?

College Athletes Should Not Have to Focus on Academics

Claire Harlin

"If America could escape the idea that college athletes are students, then the NCAA could stop running circles around scholastic requirements and get back to reality."

In the following viewpoint Claire Harlin claims that college athletes should not be expected to focus on academics. She claims that the scholastic requirements of the National Collegiate Athletic Association (NCAA) have no teeth but merely pretend to set rigorous standards and enforce them. Harlin believes that college sports stars who are focused on becoming professional athletes should not have to pretend to take an interest in academics, and neither should their coaches nor the NCAA. In 2007, Harlin was editor in chief of the *Daily Texan*, the student newspaper of the University of Texas at Austin.

AS YOU READ, CONSIDER THE FOLLOWING QUESTIONS:
1. The author claims that the National Basketball Association (NBA) wants young players to wait how long after high school before going professional?
2. What is the national average graduation rate for college athletes, according to Harlin?
3. According to Harlin, should any college athletes be considered students?

Amerrica should stop trying to worry about putting the "student" in "student-athlete."

"Student" Athletes

High school athletes vie for university team positions, and some college athletes dedicate their lives to their sports. I don't blame those who put little thought into an academic career between training and games.

To me, sports are about as exciting as unsalted popcorn, but even I got a kick out of last Wednesday night's men's basketball game [January 2009]. A young freshman made Texas basketball history when he scored 37 points and made 23 rebounds. The standing record was 30 points and 20 rebounds.

I am no sports expert, but that's pretty amazing—especially for a first-year college student.

But we can't really call Kevin Durant, a college of education freshman, a student—nor should we refer to him as an education major. He would probably not oppose being called what was probably his childhood dream: a basketball superstar.

Durant's case is starker still: The biggest reason he's not in the NBA [National Basketball Association] right now is because the league's

FAST FACT

Kevin Durant played college basketball for the 2006–2007 school year at the University of Texas, beginning his professional basketball career in the NBA in 2007 at the age of eighteen.

commissioner urged the players' union to force rising stars to wait at least one season before playing in the NBA.

Scholastic Requirements

The NCAA [National Collegiate Athletic Association] has fought for years to maintain the image of the student-athlete, whether through implementing measures such as the Student-Athlete Bill of Rights or raising the academic standards for college athletes. In 2005, for example, the NCAA approved a plan mandating that schools must graduate 50 percent of their athletes or face losing scholarships.

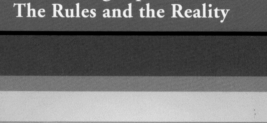

College Sports: The Rules and the Reality

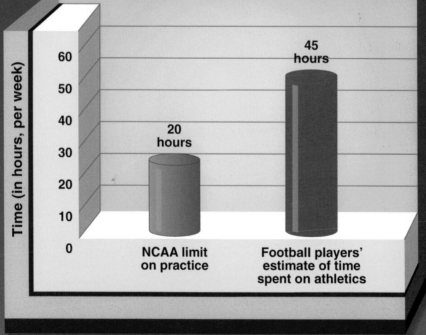

Taken from: Justin Pope, "NCAA Athletes Work Long Hours, Survey Says," *Diverse Issues in Higher Education*, September 4, 2009.

Before University of Texas freshman basketball star Kevin Durant could play in the NBA he had to sit out a season because of league rules.

In November [2008], the NCAA released figures compiled from government data showing UT's [University of Texas] athletes at a 58 percent graduation rate, trailing behind the 63 percent national average. Only two months prior to the release of that data, the association released study results showing that only 40 percent of UT football players and 44 percent of basketball players finished college between 1996 and 1999.

But study results, even if unquantifiable, don't really matter. Last time the NCAA handed out penalties, less than 2 percent of colleges actually lost scholarships.

If the NCAA isn't cutting corners when conducting its studies or computing its data, there's still a motive for athletes and coaches to cut corners to meet scholastic requirements and keep sports stars in the game.

I bet Durant's participation in a 300-person introductory class isn't on coaches' minds. And an athletic phenomenon has no good reason to be worried about class when he's at the top of the list for getting picked for the NBA, which would mean leaving UT for an eight-figure salary.

College Athletes as Students

If America could escape the idea that college athletes are students, then the NCAA could stop running circles around scholastic requirements and get back to reality. After all, a minimum SAT score of 400 for entering freshman athletes is not going to bring "students" looking for an enriching academic experience. You get close to a 400 for filling out your name properly.

Many athletes are indeed students with future plans beyond college sports, and they carry the greatest weight in keeping graduation rates up. The rest just want to play ball.

No harm is done when college athletes such as Durant don't graduate. Just like every other student, star athletes are achieving their goals, working hard and setting an example for many. Not to mention that they are bringing in big bucks for their universities.

College is a place for engineers and scholars, but being a "professional" doesn't require a degree. Durant is a young basketball player who will surely rise to professional ranks. If he decides to be held accountable for academic requirements after he's lived his dream, so be it.

Viewpoint
5

The State University Focus on Athletics Harms Academics

William C. Dowling

"When the only thing that matters at a university is big-time sports, the symbolic center of the institution has been shifted profoundly."

In the following viewpoint William C. Dowling claims that the emphasis on college sports within the university is harming the academic mission of the institution. In particular, Dowling claims that the obsession with sports at state universities prevents poor students from getting a college education and prevents all students from getting the best education they could be getting if academics were the central focus. Dowling is a professor of English and American literature at Rutgers University, the state university of New Jersey located in New Brunswick. He is the author of *Confessions of a Spoilsport: My Life and Hard Times Fighting Sports Corruption at an Old Eastern University.*

L ast week [September 25–28, 2007] the president and athletics
director of Rutgers University launched what *The Wall Street Journal* called "a campaign of character assassination against
an English professor who is a critic of the university's emphasis on
'high-stakes athletics.'"

I'm that English professor.

Sports in the University

Here's the remark that prompted the controversy: "If you were giving a scholarship to an intellectually brilliant kid who happens to play
a sport, that's fine. But they give it to a functional illiterate who can't
read a cereal box, and then make him spend 50 hours a week on physical skills. That's not opportunity. If you want to give financial help
to minorities, go find the ones who are at the library after school."

Since I've answered elsewhere the contemptible charge of "racism"
made by [president of Rutgers University] Richard McCormick and
[then-director of athletics at Rutgers University] Robert Mulcahy, let
me say a word about the deeper stakes involved in their attempt to
deliver a crude payback for *Confessions of a Spoilsport*, a book I've just
published about the damage professionalized Division I-A sports is
doing to Rutgers as an old and distinguished university.

In that book, I quote a remark made by Ohio State running back
Maurice Clarett: "The only thing that matters at Ohio State is football."
When the only thing that matters at a university is big-time sports, the
symbolic center of the institution has been shifted profoundly. Sooner
or later, everyone at the university becomes aware of the change.

When every institutional resource is dedicated and known to be
dedicated to the support and celebration of specialized physical skills,

intellectual talent and the pursuit of learning come to be disregarded and displaced, even, at many schools, despised.

In the world of Division I-A institutions, it's the [incarcerated former college football player] Maurice Claretts and [professional football player and ex-convict] Michael Vicks who are real. The student who comes to college hoping to learn about Renaissance poetry or molecular biology walks the campus as a ghost.

The single biggest problem in contemporary American higher education concerns bright students from less-than-wealthy backgrounds who just miss admission to the most competitive colleges and can't afford the costs of private universities with high academic rank. For these students in my book I call them "America's missing million" the only practical choice is their state university.

Rutgers University president Richard McCormick has received criticism from faculty for losing top New Jersey students due to sports recruiting policies.

Betraying a Promise

Here's where the sports-dominated state university betrays its promise to teach the public's children, not just the brightest students who are marginalized and neglected in favor of star athletes, but thousands of others whose own education would be incomparably richer if intellectually talented students were put at the symbolic center of the institution's values.

When bright students flee to other colleges because of a school's Division I-A sports emphasis, remedial courses proliferate and standards in regular courses begin to sag. In the classroom, where a core group of highly talented students would otherwise provide intellectual energy and incentive to more average undergraduates, very bright students find themselves isolated and suspect.

Above-average students find themselves absorbed into the mass of unmotivated or disruptive undergraduates who are now so prominent a presence in public university classrooms.

When the big-time sports ethos of athletes and boosters breeds drunkenness, violence and defiant crudity, impressionable young people, joining in because they fear being left out, lose an educational experience that could lift their lives to something better.

In the immediate background of Division I-A athletics as they exist today, in short, may be glimpsed a violated ideal of democratic education: the belief that intellectually engaged students from less-than-wealthy backgrounds deserve an education worthy of their talents.

> **FAST FACT**
>
> Rutgers, the state university of New Jersey, recently expanded the Rutgers Scarlet Knights' football stadium for a total cost of $102 million.

Avoiding the Sports Factory

President McCormick and Athletic Director Mulcahy are eager to tell you that applications are up at Rutgers, and to claim this as a result of their big-time sports program. What they won't tell you is that applications are up all over the country simply due to a temporary demo-

"I could have gone to college on an athletic scholarship, but they found out I could read."

graphic bulge in the college-age population. Nor will they tell you that research has shown that applicants attracted to a school because of a winning sports program are overwhelmingly drawn from those with low academic achievement and even lower intellectual motivation.

Today, Rutgers is losing large numbers of top New Jersey students who will do anything they can to avoid winding up at a sports factory. For the ones who make the mistake of coming anyway, Rutgers is likely to be a grim awakening.

Every semester bright students come to me, asking for letters of recommendation so they can transfer out of Rutgers. Knowing what I know and seeing what I have seen, how can I not write those letters?

But every time I see another bright and intellectually engaged student leaving for Columbia or NYU [New York University] or the University of Chicago, I can't help but feel it as a tragic loss not just for myself as a classroom teacher, but for Rutgers as an institution and New Jersey as a state.

EVALUATING THE AUTHORS' ARGUMENTS:

In this viewpoint Dowling claims that the focus on athletics within the university harms the academic mission. What does Mulcahy, author of the next viewpoint, argue in dispute of this claim?

Universities Can Successfully Balance Athletics and Academics

Robert E. Mulcahy

"The facts about Rutgers football clearly show that the program is successfully balancing athletic and academic excellence."

In the following viewpoint Robert E. Mulcahy attempts to dispute critics who claim that a focus on college football detracts from academics. Mulcahy argues that the success of the Rutgers Scarlet Knights football team on the field, along with the success of the athletes off the field, shows that athletics and academics can coexist harmoniously. He claims that not only do big sports at the university not detract from academics but also that top sports programs can help shine the spotlight on the academic achievements of the university. Mulcahy was the director of athletics at Rutgers University, the state university of New Jersey located in New Brunswick, until he was fired in 2008.

B y every measure, the Rutgers University football program is enjoying unprecedented success, both on and off the field.

You can feel the excitement across New Jersey. There's a buzz about the team among Rutgers students, faculty, staff and alumni. Record crowds jam Rutgers Stadium. Scarlet R's proliferate in the windows of cars, homes and businesses around the state.

Athletic and Academic Excellence

And yet there is a small but vocal group of people who say they are troubled by the team's success. Some of them are the same critics who ridiculed the football team's performance for years. Now they refuse to recognize that outstanding academics and athletics can coexist at Rutgers, one of the nation's premier public research universities.

FAST FACT

In the 2010 *U.S. News & World Report* national universities ranking, Rutgers is ranked sixty-sixth out of hundreds of universities in America.

Instead, they claim—absurdly—that one out-of-state bowl appearance and an eight-game winning streak have turned Rutgers into a football "factory" that is suddenly shortchanging the university's 240-year commitment to academic excellence.

The facts about Rutgers football clearly show that the program is successfully balancing athletic and academic excellence.

To better assess the academic progress of student-athletes in colleges and universities across the nation, the National Collegiate Athletic Association [NCAA] has a new standard: the Academic Progress Rate, which measures the progress of student-athletes toward their degrees. In 2005, the first year that the NCAA released this new, widely praised standard, the Rutgers football program was ranked fourth in the nation in academic progress among all 119 Division 1-A schools, behind only Stanford, Navy and Duke.

Since Greg Schiano became Rutgers' head football coach in 2001, not a single football player has left the team due to poor academic performance.

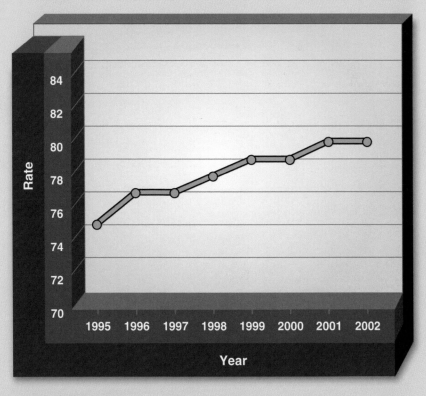

Taken from: NCAA Research Staff, "Eight-Year Trends in Federal Graduation Rates and Graduate Success Rates at NCAA Division I Institutions," November 2009.

Sports Draw Attention

For the first time in 30 years, Rutgers' football team has been ranked among the nation's top 25 programs. The football team is on track to set a home attendance record, averaging nearly 40,000 fans a game. The last two home games [October 2006] are already sold out.

The team also will compete on national or regional television at least 10 times this season—the most TV appearances in a single football season in Rutgers' history. These telecasts provide outstanding opportunities for millions of people across the nation to learn about Rutgers and our many areas of academic and athletic excellence.

Three years ago, *Sports Illustrated* published an article headlined "Why Can't Rutgers Ever Win?" A recent issue of *SI* featured a cover story on the Rutgers football team's success this season.

This success has focused unprecedented national attention on the university, which, I am told by my Rutgers colleagues, is sparking greater interest by the news media beyond New Jersey about the university's many academic accomplishments that directly benefit humanity, including new initiatives to rehabilitate stroke victims, protect oceans and promote religious coexistence.

Rutgers University gets a lot of public exposure by having a top-rated college team. This kind of exposure leads high school students from all over the country to apply to the school.

Like it or not, the success of a Top 25 program can shine a national spotlight on a university's academic accomplishments.

Colleges with Strong Athletics and Academics

Many of Rutgers' peer public research institutions have spent decades nurturing academics and athletics. These include the Georgia Institute of Technology (1990 co-national football champion), the University of Michigan (1997 co-national football champion) and the University of Texas (2005 national football champion). Each of these institutions is ranked consistently among the nation's top public research universities.

Like these peers, Rutgers can now boast a top-ranked football team and top-ranked academic programs. The university still has one of the world's finest philosophy departments. Rutgers also continues to enjoy an outstanding national reputation in a wide range of academic disciplines, from history and genetics to criminal justice and women's and gender studies.

Of course, it is impossible to predict if Rutgers' undefeated football season will continue. But it's clear that those who care about the university's continued commitment to academic excellence have good reason to applaud a second consecutive winning season.

EVALUATING THE AUTHORS' ARGUMENTS:

In this viewpoint Mulcahy argues that athletics and academics can successfully coexist within the university. Which of the previous authors in this chapter would agree with Mulcahy and which would disagree? Explain your answer.

Facts About Sports and Athletes

Editor's note: These facts can be used in reports or papers to reinforce or add credibility when making important points or claims.

Favorite Sport Among U.S. Adult Sports Fans
According to a 2008 Gallup poll:
   Forty-one percent favor football;
   10 percent, baseball;
   9 percent, basketball;
   4 percent, ice hockey;
   3 percent, soccer;
   3 percent, auto racing;
   2 percent, golf;
   2 percent, boxing;
   1 percent, tennis;
   1 percent, ice/figure skating;
   1 percent, gymnastics;
   1 percent, volleyball.

Favorite Sports Athlete Among U.S. Adult Sports Fans
According to a 2007 Harris poll, favorite athletes rank as follows:
   1. Tiger Woods, professional golfer
   2. Derek Jeter, professional baseball player
   3. Michael Jordan, professional basketball player
   4. Brett Favre, professional football player
   5. LeBron James, professional basketball player
   6. Dale Earnhardt Jr., professional race car driver
   7. Tim Duncan, professional basketball player
   8. Peyton Manning, professional football player
   9. Kobe Bryant, professional basketball player
   10. Tom Brady, professional football player

High School Sports Participation
A 2009 study by the National Federation of State High School Associations reported that participation in high school sports has never

been higher, increasing for the twentieth consecutive year. In the 2008–2009 school year participation was as follows:

- 7,536,753 high school students participated in school sports, which constitutes 55.2 percent of students enrolled in high school.
- Of that number, 3,114,091 girls and 4,422,662 boys participated.
- From the previous year, girls' participation increased by 56,825 and boys' participation increased by 50,547.

High School Sports Popularity

The 2008–2009 Participation Survey by the National Federation of State High School Associations compiled data on the most popular sports for girls and boys:

Ten most popular sports programs for boys, by number of participants:
1. football
2. track and field
3. basketball
4. baseball
5. soccer
6. wrestling
7. cross country
8. tennis
9. golf
10. swimming and diving

Ten most popular sports programs for girls, by number of participants:
1. track and field
2. basketball
3. volleyball
4. softball
5. soccer
6. cross country
7. tennis
8. swimming and diving
9. competitive spirit squads
10. golf

Organizations to Contact

The editors have compiled the following list of organizations concerned with the issues debated in this book. The descriptions are derived from materials provided by the organizations. All have publications or information available for interested readers. The list was compiled on the date of publication of the present volume; the information provided here may change. Be aware that many organizations take several weeks or longer to respond to inquiries, so allow as much time as possible for the receipt of requested materials.

American Association of Adapted Sports Programs (AAASP)
PO Box 451047
Atlanta, GA 31145
(404) 294-0070
fax: (404) 294-5788
e-mail: sports@adaptedsports.org
Web site: www.adaptedsports.org

The AAASP supports the concept that school-based sports are a vital part of the education process of students. The association has adapted sports for the student-athlete based on functional ability, which parallels the traditional interscholastic athletic system. The AAASP provides information about several adapted sports, a video and photo gallery, and the newsletter *Adapted Sports Report*.

Athletes Against Steroids
731 Kirkman Rd.
Orlando, FL 32811
(877) 914-9910
e-mail: tomc@athletesagainststeroids.org
Web site: www.athletesagainststeroids.org

Athletes Against Steroids is an organization that discourages steroid use and aims to help those who use steroids to quit. Athletes Against Steroids uses education, research, nutritional alternatives, and addiction assistance to fight steroid use. The organization publishes the weekly newsletter *Drug Free Athlete*, as well as other information available at its Web site.

Athletes for a Better World (ABW)
1740 Barnesdale Way NE
Atlanta, GA 30309
(404) 892-2328
Web site: www.abw.org

The mission of ABW is to use sports to develop character, teamwork, and citizenship through commitment to an athletic Code for Living. This Code for Living encourages discipline, integrity, respect, cooperation, and compassion in the sport environment. The organization provides free educational materials about the Code for Living, available at its Web site.

Canadian Centre for Ethics in Sport (CCES)
350-955 Green Valley Crescent
Ottawa, ON K2C 3V4, CANADA
(613) 521-3340
fax: (613) 521-3134
e-mail: info@cces.ca
Web site: www.cces.ca

Born out of a merger between the Canadian Centre for Drug-Free Sport and Fair Play Canada, the CCES is founded on the principles of fair play and drug-free sport. CCES promotes ethical conduct in sport using a comprehensive approach that includes research, advocacy and promotion, prevention, policy development, and detection and deterrence. CCES publishes numerous informational pamphlets, including *Bullying Prevention in Sports*.

National Alliance for Youth Sports (NAYS)
2050 Vista Pkwy.
West Palm Beach, FL 33411
(800) 729-2057
fax: (561) 684-2546
e-mail: nays@nays.org
Web site: www.nays.org

The NAYS is a nonprofit organization that advocates for positive and safe sports and activities for youth. It offers programs and services for everyone involved in youth sports experiences, including professional administrators, volunteer administrators, volunteer coaches, officials, parents, and young athletes. It publishes the magazine *SportingKid.*

National Coalition Against Violent Athletes (NCAVA)

PO Box 620453
Littleton, CO 80162
(720) 963-0373
e-mail: info@ncava.org
Web site: www.ncava.org

NCAVA works to educate the public on a variety of issues regarding athletes and violent behavior, while also providing support to the victims. NCAVA strives to promote positive athlete development through education, support, and accountability. NCAVA provides news, links, and articles at its Web site, including the article "Male Abuse Victims Suffer from Crime and Stereotypes."

National Collegiate Athletic Association (NCAA)

700 W. Washington St., PO Box 6222
Indianapolis, IN 46206-6222
(317) 917-6222
fax: (317) 917-6888
Web site: www.ncaa.org

The NCAA is a voluntary organization through which the nation's colleges and universities govern their athletics programs. The purpose of the NCAA is to govern competition in a fair, safe, equitable, and sportsmanlike manner, and to integrate intercollegiate athletics into higher education so that the educational experience of the student-athlete is paramount. The NCAA publishes the quarterly magazine *Champion* and other publications, including *Student-Athlete Race and Ethnicity Report.*

Sport in Society

Northeastern University
360 Huntington Ave., 510 INV

Boston, MA 02115
(617) 373-4025
fax: (617) 373-4566
e-mail: sportinsociety@neu.edu
Web site: www.sportinsociety.org

Sport in Society aims to use the power and appeal of sport to foster diversity, prevent violence, and improve the health of local and global communities. Sport in Society uses innovative programming and extensive outreach through sports to promote diversity, prevent men's violence against women, eradicate youth violence, and improve the health of disenfranchised urban youth. The center provides research publications at its Web site, including the "Athlete Bill of Rights."

U.S. Anti-Doping Agency (USADA)
1330 Quail Lake Loop, Ste. 260
Colorado Springs, CO 80906-4651
(866) 601-2632
fax: (719) 785-2001
e-mail: webmaster@usantidoping.org
Web site: www.usantidoping.org

The USADA is the national anti-doping organization for the Olympic movement in the United States. The USADA works to preserve the integrity of competition, inspire true sport, and protect the rights of athletes in the Olympic & Paralympic movement in the United States. The USADA publishes the newsletter *Spirit of Sport* among other educational resources available at its Web site.

Women's Sports Foundation
1899 Hempstead Tpk., Ste. 400
East Meadow, NY 11554
(800) 227-3988
fax: (516) 542-4716
e-mail: info@womenssportsfoundation.org
Web site: www.womenssportsfoundation.org

Founded by tennis champion Billie Jean King in 1974, the Women's Sports Foundation strives for gender equity in sports. The Women's

Sports Foundation advocates for equality, educates the public, conducts research, and offers grants to promote sports and physical activity for girls and women. The Women's Sports Foundation publishes numerous publications, including the report *Her Life Depends on It II.*

For Further Reading

Books

Assael, Shaun. *Steroid Nation: Juiced Home Run Totals, Anti-aging Miracles, and a Hercules in Every High School; The Secret History of America's True Drug Addiction.* New York: ESPN Books, 2007. Chronicles steroid use beginning with the bodybuilders of Venice Beach in the 1970s, continuing through to the NFL's Raiders of the 1980s and 1990s, to the baseball scandals of the twenty-first century.

Blumenthal, Karen. *Let Me Play: The Story of Title IX: The Law That Changed the Future of Girls in America.* New York: Atheneum, 2005. Recounts the efforts of lawmakers, teachers, parents, and athletes who played a role in ensuring that Title IX was passed, protected, and enforced.

Burgos, Adrian, Jr. *Playing America's Game: Baseball, Latinos, and the Color Line.* Berkeley and Los Angeles: University of California Press, 2007. Tells the story of the Latino men who negotiated the color line in professional baseball from the 1880s to the present, passing as Spanish in the major leagues or seeking acceptance in the Negro leagues.

Depauw, Karen P., and Susan J. Gavron. *Disability Sport.* Champaign, IL: Human Kinetics, 2005. Provides a comprehensive and practical look at the past, present, and future of disability sport, with in-depth coverage of the essential issues involving athletes with disabilities.

Fainaru-Wada, Mark, and Lance Williams. *Game of Shadows: Barry Bonds, BALCO, and the Steroids Scandal That Rocked Professional Sports.* New York: Gotham, 2007. Two *San Francisco Chronicle* reporters provide an account of the steroids scandal that made headlines across the country, exposing the secrets of the BALCO investigation.

Finley, Peter, and Laura Finley. *The Sports Industry's War on Athletes.* Santa Barbara, CA: Praeger, 2006. Confronts the many problems facing athletics today and provides recommendations for improving the sports environment in America.

Gerdy, John R. *Air Ball: American Education's Failed Experiment with Elite Athletics.* Jackson: University Press of Mississippi, 2006. Argues that the American system of school and community athletics is broken, and offers a blueprint for reforming athletics.

Ginsburg, Richard D., and Stephen Durant, with Amy Baltzell. *Whose Game Is It, Anyway?* New York: Houghton Mifflin, 2006. Two youth sports psychologists and a former Olympic athlete provide guidance for parents to maximize the benefits that sports have to offer while avoiding the many pitfalls.

Lapchick, Richard E., ed. *New Game Plan for College Sport.* Lanham, MD: Rowman & Littlefield Education, 2006. Critical issues in intercollegiate sport examined from a variety of perspectives, including the commercialization of sport, race and gender, performance-enhancing drugs, and the academic peril faced by student athletes.

McDonagh, Eileen, and Laura Pappano. *Playing with the Boys: Why Separate Is Not Equal in Sports.* New York: Oxford University Press, 2007. Uses examples from the world of contemporary American athletics to argue that women have been unfairly excluded from participating in sports on an equal footing with men.

McMahon, Regan. *Revolution in the Bleachers: How Parents Can Take Back Family Life in a World Gone Crazy over Youth Sports.* New York: Gotham, 2007. A journalist and mother of two athletic kids exposes the physical and emotional dangers of our over-the-top youth sports culture, and offers practical solutions for positive change.

Porterfield, Jason. *Doping: Athletes and Drugs.* New York: Rosen, 2007. Explains what anabolic steroids and other performance-enhancing drugs are, describes the pressures athletes face, explores the effects of doping on young people, and discusses legal issues.

Powell, Shaun. *Souled Out? How Blacks Are Winning and Losing in Sports.* Champaign, IL: Human Kinetics, 2008. Looks at blacks' status in the sporting landscape, offering a perspective that challenges everyone to address the obstacles that remain.

Sokolove, Michael. *Warrior Girls: Protecting Our Daughters Against the Injury Epidemic in Women's Sports.* New York: Simon & Schuster, 2008. Argues that the women's sports revolution that has evolved since Title IX has created a dangerous injury epidemic among girls.

Zimbalist, Andrew. *The Bottom Line: Observations and Arguments on the Sports Business.* Philadelphia: Temple University Press, 2006. A sports economist analyzes the value of sports, examining the worth of the players and the profitability of teams, and the importance of publicly funded stadiums.

Periodicals

Abrams, Douglas E. "It's a Blessing Just to Play: Lessons for All of Us from Young Athletes of 2008," *St. Louis Post-Dispatch*, December 31, 2008.

Adelson, Andrea. "Mitchell Investigation Reveals Little About Baseball's Steroids Scandal," *Orlando Sentinel*, December 14, 2007.

Allday, Erin. "The Growing Pains of Childhood Sports Injuries," *San Francisco Chronicle*, March 7, 2008.

Anderson, Jane. "Child Injuries: Many from Sports," *Pediatric News*, August 2009.

Balko, Radley. "Should We Allow Performance Enhancing Drugs in Sports? One Argument in Favor," *Reason*, January 23, 2008.

Blue, Adrianne. "It's the Real Dope," *New Statesman*, August 14, 2006.

Broder, David. "The Sports World in Foul Territory," *Washington Post*, April 10, 2008.

Burnette, Margarette. "Play a Team Sport?" *Parenting*, March 2008.

Burton, Jim. "Baseball Will Survive Latest Round of Steroids, Greed," *Standard-Examiner* (Ogden, UT), August 5, 2009.

Burwell, Bryan. "Steroid Revelation Proves A-Rod Really Is A-Fraud," *St. Louis Post-Dispatch*, February 8, 2009.

Butland, Dale. "The Tail That Wags the Dog," *Cincinnati Post*, December 6, 2007.

Chafets, Zev. "Let Steroids into the Hall of Fame," *New York Times*, June 20, 2009.

Curtis, Bryan. "Playola: How Cheating Has Changed," *Texas Monthly*, September 2007.

Deford, Frank. "Unfair Advantage: As Title IX Turns 35, the Law Needs to Be Re-evaluated," *Sports Illustrated*, June 22, 2007.

Fried, Barbara H. "Punting Our Future: College Athletics and Admissions," *Change*, May/June 2007.

Gorman, Christine. "How We're Harming Young Athletes," *Time*, September 10, 2006.

Hayes, Reggie. "Great Athletes Are Not Perfect People," *News-Sentinel* (Fort Wayne, IN), February 6, 2009.

Hoyt, Clark. "Baseball's Top-Secret Roster," *New York Times*, August 9, 2009.

Jeansonne, John. "Baseball Needs to Come Clean About Steroids," *Newsday*, May 8, 2009.

Junior Scholastic. "Juiced Up: A Report Condemns a 'Steroids Era' in Major League Baseball," January 21, 2008.

Lewis, Andrea. "Battering Barry Bonds Deflects Our Culpability," *Progressive*, August 14, 2007.

Lilja, Nick. "Lesson in Economics," *Daily Barometer* (Corvallis, OR), July 5, 2007.

Maese, Rick. "Many Athletes Are Real Role Models," *Baltimore Sun*, August 26, 2007.

Maher, John. "Athletes Caught Between Standards," *Austin* (TX) *American-Statesman*, October 29, 2007.

Malone, Christian. "Athletes Should Be Role Models," *Valdosta* (GA) *Daily Times*, March 2, 2008.

Martino, Andy. "On Baseball: No Way to Prove Players Are Clean," *Philadelphia Inquirer*, August 23, 2009.

McCluskey, Mark. "Nix the Ban on Sports Drugs," *Wired*, September 21, 2005.

McCormick, Richard L. "Athletics and Academics: Perfect Together," *Star-Ledger* (Newark, N J), February 3, 2008.

McMahon, Regan. "Parents, Coaches Who Need Time-Outs: Adult Violence at Kids' Sports Sets a Terrible Example," *San Francisco Chronicle*, November 5, 2006.

Mink, Rob. "Athletes Should Not Be Our Role Models," *Daily Barometer* (Corvallis, OR), October 2, 2009.

Mitten, Matthew J. "Is Drug Testing of Athletes Necessary?" *USA Today* magazine, November 2005.

Mueller, Christine. "Racing to a Degree: High School Sports Help Girls Earn College Diplomas," *U.S. News & World Report*, August 6, 2007.

Pappano, Laura, and Eileen McDonagh. "Women and Men in Sports: Separate Is Not Equal," *Christian Science Monitor*, January 31, 2008.

Pollick, Josh. "College Athletes Should Be Students Too," *Daily Pennsylvanian*, January 9, 2006.

Quart, Alissa. "Girls and Boys, Interrupted," *New York Times*, October 2, 2006.

Rosenberg, Benjamin E. "Why Should Notre Dame's Football Coach Make More than Tenured Professors?" *Christian Science Monitor*, September 26, 2009.

Schneier, Bruce. "Drugs: Sports' Prisoner's Dilemma," *Wired*, August 10, 2006.

Shore, Rebecca. "How We Got Here: A Timeline of Performance-Enhancing Drugs in Sports," *Sports Illustrated*, March 11, 2008.

Springen, Karen. "Don't Go Overboard," *Newsweek*, June 18, 2007.

Steinberg, Aaron. "Mr. Brand Goes to Washington: Does the NCAA Deserve Non-profit Status?" *Reason*, January 4, 2007.

Steinberger, Mike. "U.S. College Sports Graduate to Big Business," *Financial Times*, December 16, 2005.

Sullum, Jacob. "Coping with Doping: If It's Allowed, It's Not Cheating," *Reason*, August 2, 2006.

Thompson, Adam. "Is Baseball Drug Ruling a Fourth-Amendment Foul?" *Wall Street Journal*, January 16, 2007.

Tublitz, Nathan. "Ducking Education," *Register-Guard* (Eugene, OR), January 14, 2007.

Welch, Matt. "Jock Sniffing: Congress Has No Business Examining Baseball's Urine," *Reason*, March 14, 2005.

Woody, Paul. "Off the Field, Athletes' Flaws Are Sometimes Fatal," *Richmond* (VA) *Times-Dispatch*, July 8, 2009.

Worcester, Sharon. "Girls' Sports Injury Prevention Should Be a Priority," *Pediatric News*, May 2005.

Web Sites

National College Players Association (NCPA) (www.ncpanow.org). The Web site of the NCPA has information on playing sports in college, including information about getting scholarships and committing to a school.

National Institute on Drug Abuse (NIDA) (www.nida.nih.gov). The Web site of NIDA, which is a part of the National Institutes of Health, a component of the U.S. Department of Health and Human Services, contains information about anabolic steroids.

Index

participation in, 7
time and money spent on, 18
House Government Reform
Committee, 72, 78, *79*
Housman, Robert, 71–76
Human chorionic gonadotropin
(HCG), 47–48
Hyman, Mark, 30

I
Injuries, sports-related, 19, 29, 30
Interscholastic sports, 24–25

J
John, Tommy, 56
Johnson, Steven, 56
Jones, Marion, 66–70, *68*
Juiced (Canseco), 52, 55, 60
Juicing the Game (Bryant), 59,
62, 64

K
Kendrick, Carleton, 35, 37
Knobler, Mike, 96

L
Laccetti, Silvio, 95–100
Laser eye surgery, 56
Latique, Esther, 34
Lench, Brooke de, 23–27
Lewis, Michael, 83–89
Love Me, Hate Me (Pearlman),
59, 62

M
Major League Baseball (MLB)
as big business, 74

congressional investigation of
steroid use in, 71–81
drug testing by, 55
prohibition on performance-
enhancing drugs by, 45–50
steroid use as benefit for, 52–57
widespread use of performance-
enhancing drugs in, 59–64
Mann, Windsor, 11–16
Marth, Stephen, 98
McCaffrey, Barry, 74
McCain, John, 78
McCormick, Richard, 108, *109*,
110
McGwire, Mark, 46
McIntosh, Tara, 28–31
Mitchell, George J., 80
Moyer, Jamie, 48
Mulcahy, Robert E., *97*, 108,
110, 113–117

N
National Collegiate Athletic
Association (NCAA)
academic requirements of, 87,
103–105, 115
amateur model of, 91
on commercialization of college
sports, 86
regulations of, 96
National Health and Nutrition
Examination Survey
(NHANES), 27
Novitzky, Jeff, 61

O
Obesity, 24

Congress should investigate, 71–76

Congress should not investigate, 77–81

health risks of, 72

among high school athletes, 21

public opinion on, 60

See also Performance-enhancing drugs

Stevens, Jerramy, 7–8

Super Bowl, 14

Surgery, 56

Syracuse University, 98

T

Team sports, fan identification with, 12–13

Teenagers

overweight, *25*, 27

participation in sports by, 24–25

Television, sports on, 7

U

Ueberroths, Peter, 69

University of Buffalo, 97–98

University of Washington Huskies, 7–8

U.S. Anti-Doping Agency (USADA), *73*, 74

V

Vick, Michael, *36, 40,* 42, 109

W

War, sports as substitute for, 14, 16

Weinberg, Steve, 58–64

Williams, Armstrong, 38–43

Williams, Curtis, 8

Williams, Lance, 59, 61

Wood, Daniel B., 32–37

Wood, Kerry, 56

Woods, Tiger, 29, 33–37, 39, 41, 42

Y

Young, Vince, 88–89

Youth sports

benefits of, 23–27

fun in, 30

harm caused by, 28–31

inclusive, 24–27

parental involvement in, 29–30

specialization in, 29–30

See also High school sports

Z

Zimmerman, Jonathan, 17–22

Zirin, Dave, 65–70

Picture Credits

AP Images, 36, 40, 73, 82, 87, 92, 97, 109
© Bob Jones Photography/Alamy, 53
© Mitch Diamond/Alamy, 31
© Michael Dwyer/Alamy, 13
Romeo Gusman/CSM/Landov, 116
Gary Hershorn/Reuters/Landov, 68
Chuck Kennedy/Reuters/Landov, 79
Steve Nesius/Reuters/Landov, 10
Albert Pena/CSM/Landov, 104
© Picture Partners/Alamy, 20
Ray Stubblebine/Reuters/Landov, 49
Justin Sullivan/Getty Images, 25
Victor Habbick Visions/Photo Researchers, Inc., 44
Kimberly White/Reuters/Landov, 63
Steve Zmina, 15, 19, 26, 34, 42, 47, 54, 60, 75, 85, 99, 103, 115